FROM THE KITCHENS OF

YamCHOPS™

NORTH AMERICA'S ORIGINAL VEGAN BUTCHER SHOP

Mind-Blowing Plant-Based Meat Substitutions

Michael Abramson

Chef and Founder of YamChops

PAGE STREET
PUBLISHING CO.

PAGE STREET
PUBLISHING CO.

First published in 2018 by

Page Street Publishing Co.

27 Congress Street, Suite 105

Salem, MA 01970

www.pagestreetpublishing.com

Distributed by Macmillan, sales in Canada by The Canadian Manda Group.

22 21 20 19 18   1 2 3 4 5

ISBN-13: 978-1-62414-488-2

ISBN-10: 1-62414-488-8

Library of Congress Control Number: 2017953245

Cover and book design by Page Street Publishing Co.

Photography by Vincenzo Pistritto

Printed and bound in China

Dedication

This cookbook is dedicated to three amazing women who joined in the dream called YamChops—my wife Toni and my daughters, Jess and Leya—and to dreams coming true!

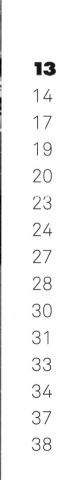

CONTENTS

THERE'S AN APP FOR THAT—SELFIE-WORTHY APPETIZERS AND SIDES

ACE IN THE BOWL—BOLD BOWLS, BROTHS AND BREWS

INTRODUCTION

"What the heck is a vegan butcher anyway?"

More than any other question, we're asked, "What are you?"

Yup, even more often than, "Where do you get your protein?"

In the simplest of responses, YamChops prepares center-of-the-plate protein alternatives that are all plant-based, and we do so in a butcher shop format.

Some might say that a vegan butcher is an oxymoron, but we believe plant-based proteins can (and should) be staples of any kitchen or diet. Our recipes appeal to all types of eaters: vegans, vegetarians and flexitarians—those who are choosing to reduce their meat and dairy consumption. As you'll see, we have had a lot of fun and take some creative license when we turn a commonly understood animal protein on its head by recreating it as a plant-based protein instead.

Let me take you on a bit of a trip back in time to describe how YamChops came to be. Growing up, I vividly remember countless weekend visits to my grandparents who lived in Regina. My grandfather immigrated to Canada from Romania in 1928. Among the many things he did to build a new life, my grandfather was a livestock trader. He'd travel to the remote flatlands of Saskatchewan, bargaining with farmers for a cow to bring to Regina's livestock auction. Being religious, he wouldn't travel on the Sabbath, so my grandparents often had a cow as their guest for the weekend—many times on the same weekends that we were visiting. All of the cows, coincidently, were named Bessie. For years I believed that it was the same cow, until my grandfather thought that it would be a great experience for his nine-year-old grandson if he took me to a cattle auction. I didn't quite understand what was going on at the stockyards, but I remember feeling his pride when he was showing me around the yard, his excitement when Bessie was being paraded around the auction ring, and his elation when he was handed a check.

This is my first memory of what it means to bring passion and celebration to what you do. In later years, it also became my first memory of animal consciousness—but at the time, all I took in was his unbelievable spirit in doing what he did to provide for his family.

I fully embraced a plant-based lifestyle when I was nineteen. At the time, I was pursuing a special education degree at the University of Windsor and working at a residential school for autistic children. Prepared plant-based choices back then were pretty sparse, as was my food budget, so I figured I best learn how to cook a few dishes, because living on French fries was not going to work long term.

It didn't take long for me to discover that cooking was not only a joy, but that I could make stuff taste great as well. While preparing great tasting food was the ultimate reward, I found that I was falling in love with the whole process: going to the farmer's market, discovering and experimenting with stuff I've never seen before, fusing multiple cuisine styles and creating food that made people smile.

After two years in Windsor and a stint at the University of Lund, Sweden, I moved back to Toronto and met Toni. For our first date I took her to The Cow Café—one of Toronto's few veg restaurants at the time. Then, when she found out that I could cook and was pretty manic about cleanliness, she knew I was the man for her.

Time went on, we married and we opened our advertising agency theadlibgroup in 1985—an agency that we ran for almost three decades. Along the way we were given the two greatest gifts of our lives—our daughters Jess and Leya (who have since given us the gift of our grandkids Kaya, Ollin and Rayne).

From the time the girls were old enough to stand on a stool, they joined me in the kitchen and we cooked and we cooked and we cooked. This was, and thirty years later still is, the ultimate daddy-daughter time for me!

Around 2009, I decided it was time to see if I could take my cooking to a new level, and I completed my first professional certification in Natural Foods, Vegetarian and Vegan. It was a good and a bad thing. Good in that it really did give me the confidence to take my cooking up a notch; bad because it made me itch to get more seriously into food from all aspects.

A year later, this crazy idea of opening a food business started to dance around my mind. Three years later, we were approached by another ad agency, and we ultimately struck a deal to sell theadlibgroup. The stars were aligned. All that was left to do was to convince the love of my life that fifty-nine was the perfect age to open a plant-based business.

The concept of a plant-based butcher shop offering prepared foods was born. And on June 9, 2014, YamChops opened its doors. I'll never forget Toni, Jess, Leya and I staring in disbelief at the line of people waiting for us to open our doors.

We felt pretty confident that Toronto's vegan and vegetarian world would give a plant-based butcher shop a shot, and we hoped that we would appeal to flexitarians as well. Now, more than half of our guests are flex. Fact is, we don't judge people's choices when they visit YamChops. We fully understand that some people take a little longer to adopt a plant-based diet than others. For us, we figured that the easiest way to convince them of the merits of a plant-based diet is to feed them, to show them that vegan is delicious and to demonstrate that compassion not only feels great but tastes great too.

From day one, we were (and still are) humbled by the media attention that we received and continue to receive from around the world. We are proud to raise the plant-based message—for our health, for our planet's health and for our animal's health.

Among the many highlights of all this media attention was an invitation we received nine months after we opened to appear on Canada's number-one-rated *Dragons' Den*, an investment-style reality TV show. We were being invited to appear on *Dragons' Den*!

We knew we didn't even have a full year under our belts. We knew we didn't have a growth plan in place. We knew that we didn't know the answers to many of the questions that the Dragons commonly asked. We knew that we weren't profitable at that point. And . . . we also knew that there was no possible way that we would turn down the opportunity to appear on national television to spread the plant-based message and the YamChops message.

So we got busy. We had only fifteen days to prepare for our filming, and we had lots to do! We got our books in order with projections for the remainder of the year. We devised a growth plan that culminated in fifty YamChops franchise locations in North America within five years. We agreed on what we were going to ask for from the Dragons and what percentage we would be willing to give up. We decided on what we were going to feed the Dragons. We invited friends and business colleagues to play the role of Dragons and held a mock filming. We designed a set that emulated our store.

We were as ready as we were going to be.

And then we were there. Jess, Toni and I standing on the stage, facing five Dragons, telling them the YamChops story, feeding them some YamChops goodies and asking them to invest in us.

We weren't sure if the Dragons were going to love to eat vegan—or if they were going to love to eat vegans! To our relief, they loved to eat vegan. They loved our food, our concept, our branding and our story, and one of the Dragons, Jim Treliving, offered us an investment deal.

Ultimately, we didn't close the deal with Jim. In the months that followed our taping, we quickly realized that we weren't ready at that point to bring YamChops to market. We still had a lot to do to become franchise ready. Over the next year, we got busy getting ready. And, when we were, we knew we wanted to partner with an established franchise organization because bringing a new brand to market is more than Toni and I were ready, willing or able to do on our own.

Many investors and franchise organizations contacted us after our *Dragons' Den* appearance, but only one shared our passion and our commitment to the plant-based movement. In August of 2016, we partnered with Vancouver-based Scott Bender and Lawrence Eade of Box Concepts Group. Six months later, we began franchising YamChops and, at the time of this writing (August 2017), we have two locations set to open in Vancouver and two additional locations set to open in Toronto, and we've established a second food production facility in Vancouver.

It has truly been an amazing three years! We are honored to play a role in advancing plant-based eating and humbled by the attention that we've received.

For our health. For our environment. For our animals.

Richard

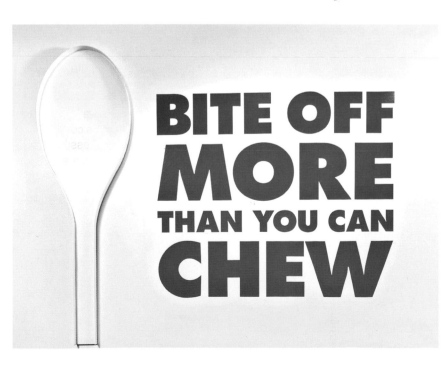

BITE OFF MORE THAN YOU CAN CHEW

Chapter 1

STEP UP TO THE PLATE

Mouthwatering Meatless Mains

From plant-based Chick*n Schnitzel (page 14) to Korean BBQ Ribs (page 37) to Carrot Not Dogs (page 27) to No-Crab Crab Cakes (page 38)—these recipes delight thousands upon thousands of guests at YamChops. These are the dishes that helped make YamChops famous!

Chick*n Schnitzel

I grew up in Winnipeg, and our special occasion treat way back then was a family dinner at our local schnitzel house. (Actually, back then, I think it was Winnipeg's only schnitzel house.) So schnitzel is definitely a childhood fave, but here it's gone vegan! Grab yourself a big, crusty, round bun and load it up with a Chick*n Schnitzel, tomato sauce, sautéed mushrooms, caramelized onions and pickled jalapeño. Open wide and join me on a trip down memory lane.

. . . .

1½ cups (350 g) canned chickpeas

3 tbsp (45 ml) olive oil

1 tbsp (12 g) almond butter or tahini

1 cup (155 g) vital wheat gluten

1 cup (119 g) bread crumbs, regular or Italian flavor, plus more for breading

½ cup (120 ml) vegetable stock

3 tbsp (45 ml) tamari or soy sauce

2 tsp (5 g) Hungarian paprika

1 tsp dried thyme leaves

1 tsp dried sage leaves

1 tsp garlic powder

All-purpose flour

2 tbsp (30 ml) egg replacer, plus more for breading

6 tbsp (90 ml) water

Grape-seed or canola oil, for frying

Rinse the chickpeas and drain them well. Add the chickpeas to a food processor and pulse 3 or 4 times. Add the olive oil and almond butter and pulse in 4-second intervals until the chickpeas are coarsely mashed. You want to keep some of the texture of the chickpeas, but you don't want pieces that are bigger than a peppercorn. You are not going for a smooth hummus consistency. Be sure to scrape down the sides of the processor and mix the contents with a rubber spatula a couple of times during the process.

Empty the chickpea mixture into the bowl of a stand mixer fitted with the paddle attachment. Add the gluten, bread crumbs, stock, tamari, paprika, thyme, sage and garlic powder and mix on low speed for 5 minutes. Move the mixture to a clean countertop and knead by hand for an additional 3 minutes. The mixture should be slightly wet but not at all sticky. If it's too wet, knead in an additional 1 to 2 teaspoons (2.5 to 5 g) of the bread crumbs. If it's too dry, knead in an additional 1 to 2 teaspoons (5 to 10 ml) of stock.

Tear off a golf ball-size piece of dough and roll it into a ball. With both thumbs on top of the ball, gently pull the dough apart in opposite directions. If the dough has a fibrous texture when you pull it apart, you're good to go. If it does not, knead it for another 3 or 4 minutes. Let the dough rest, lightly covered with a clean towel, for 30 minutes on your countertop.

Once the dough has rested, measure off pieces weighing 2½ to 3½ ounces (80 to 100 g). Press them flat on a lightly floured countertop and, using a rolling pin, roll them to approximately 1/8-inch (3-mm)-thick patties (schnitzels).

Set up a breading station with 1 flat bowl containing unbleached, all-purpose flour, 1 flat bowl containing the egg replacer and water, whisked together well and 1 flat bowl containing bread crumbs.

Place about ½ inch (13 mm) of grape-seed oil in a skillet and heat it over medium heat. Lightly dust one schnitzel in the flour, submerge it in the egg replacer mixture and bread it in the bread crumbs, patting the bread crumbs onto the surface of the schnitzel with your dry hand. Place the breaded schnitzel in the oil and cook until golden brown on the bottom, approximately 60 to 70 seconds. Carefully flip the schnitzel and cook until the second side is golden brown. Remove the schnitzel to a paper towel lined plate to drain. Continue until all of the schnitzel are breaded and fried.

Keep warm in a 200°F (93°C) oven until ready to serve.

Beet Wellington

At YamChops, we regularly feature this elaborate main dish on our Christmas dinner menu . . . just another reason for us to look forward to the arrival of Saint Nick. It's a savory puff pastry pocket stuffed with roasted beets, mushroom-walnut meat and red onion relish. Top it off with our Shiitake Miso Gravy (page 151) and there'll be no beef at your holiday table this year!

. . . .

2 lb (900 g) red beets (see notes), washed and dried

1½ tbsp (22 ml) olive oil

½ tsp sea salt

½ tsp freshly ground black pepper

1 (14-oz [397-g]) package vegan puff pastry, thawed (see notes)

Vegan butter, melted

Mushroom-Walnut Meat

1 tbsp (15 g) vegan butter

3 cups (225 g) cremini or brown mushrooms, finely chopped

1½ tsp (2 g) minced fresh thyme

1½ tsp (2 g) minced fresh rosemary

3 small cloves garlic, minced

1 medium shallot, peeled and minced

⅔ cup (100 g) walnut pieces, roughly chopped

2 tbsp (30 ml) vegetable stock

2 tbsp (30 ml) red wine

Red Onion Relish

2 tbsp (30 ml) olive oil

1½ lb (680 g) red onion, peeled and thinly sliced

½ tsp sea salt

¼ tsp freshly ground black pepper

½ cup (100 g) organic cane sugar

¼ cup (60 ml) sherry vinegar

½ tsp red chili flakes

¼ tsp ground allspice

Preheat the oven to 400°F (204°C).

To prepare the roasted beets, trim the root and tip ends and place the beets in the center of a large sheet of aluminum foil. Drizzle with the olive oil and sprinkle with the salt and pepper. Tightly wrap the beets in the aluminum foil, and place the package on a lined baking sheet in the oven for 45 to 60 minutes. The cooking time will vary depending on the size of the beets. The beets are ready when they are easily pierced with a skewer or the tip of a knife.

Remove the beets from the oven. Carefully unwrap the aluminum foil and allow the beets to cool. When the beets are cool enough to handle, peel them and slice into ¼-inch (6-mm)-thick rounds. Set aside.

To prepare the mushroom-walnut meat, heat the butter in a large sauté pan over medium heat. Once the butter has melted, add the mushrooms, fresh herbs, garlic and shallot. Sauté, stirring often, until the mushrooms are tender, approximately 6 to 8 minutes. Add the walnuts, vegetable stock and red wine to the mushrooms. Continue to cook for 10 to 12 minutes until most of the liquid cooks off. Remove from the heat and allow the mixture to cool.

To prepare the red onion relish, heat the olive oil in a large sauté pan over low heat. Add the sliced onions and cook, stirring often, until the onions are soft but not darkly caramelized, approximately 25 to 30 minutes. The cooking time will vary depending on the thickness of your slices.

Sprinkle the salt, pepper and sugar over the onions and stir well. Cover the pan and cook for an additional 10 minutes. Stir in the sherry vinegar, red chili flakes and allspice. Raise the heat to medium and cook for an additional 20 to 25 minutes, stirring regularly, until most of the liquid has cooked off. Place the onions in a bowl and set aside to cool.

Preheat the oven to 375°F (190°C).

(continued)

Beet Wellington (Cont.)

Unwrap the thawed puff pastry and gently roll it out with a rolling pin until the dough is approximately ⅛-inch (3-mm)-thick. Cut the dough into 4 squares, approximately 7 × 7 inches (178 × 178 mm) each. Working with one square at a time, layer one-fourth of the beets, one-fourth of the red onion relish and one-fourth of the mushroom mixture on the dough, leaving a 1½-inch (38-mm) border around all of the edges. Brush the border with water and gently fold the puff pastry over the filling to form a tight, sealed package. Repeat with the remaining puff pastry squares.

Place the assembled puff pastry packages on a parchment lined sheet pan and lightly brush with melted vegan butter. Bake until they're puffed and golden brown, approximately 30 to 35 minutes.

These Beet Wellingtons are delicious paired with our Shiitake Miso Gravy (page 151).

Notes: At YamChops, we form these bundles of deliciousness using mini loaf pans as a mold. Drape the puff pastry over the loaf pan and gently push the dough into the cavity. Leave sufficient dough overlapping the sides and ends of the loaf pan so you can fold it over the filling and seal the edges. Then fill it up with the beets, red onion relish and mushroom-walnut meat. Seal and gently turn the package onto a sheet pan.

To avoid staining when working with red beets, wear plastic gloves and cover your work area with plastic wrap.

Most puff pastry dough is accidently vegan, but carefully check the ingredients to be sure.

Teriyaki Chick*n

A little salty, a little sweet and highlighted with ginger and star anise, this sauce is ready in less than 20 minutes and way better than your local Chinese takeout.

. . . .

Teriyaki Sauce

1 cup (240 ml) water

5 tbsp (62 g) brown sugar

¼ cup (60 ml) tamari or soy sauce

2 tbsp (30 ml) agave syrup

1½ tsp (4 g) ginger powder

¼ tsp garlic powder

1 star anise pod

1 tbsp (10 g) cornstarch mixed with 3 tbsp (45 ml) water

Chick*n

2 tbsp (30 ml) grape-seed or canola oil

1 recipe Plant-Based Chick*n (page 69) cut into ⅜ x ⅜ x 3-inch (9 x 9 x 76-mm) strips (or substitute your favorite vegan chick*n strips)

1 sweet onion, cut into ¼-inch (6-mm) half moon slices

1 red pepper, cut into ¼-inch (6-mm) slices

1 large carrot, cut into ⅛-inch (3-mm) coins

1 small head broccoli, broken into florets

½ cup (120 ml) water

Whisk together the water, brown sugar, tamari, agave, ginger powder, garlic powder and star anise pod in a pot over medium heat. Cook, whisking regularly, until the sugar melts and the sauce reaches a light boil, approximately 4 to 5 minutes.

Whisk the cornstarch and water together in a small bowl to form a slurry. Slowly pour the slurry into the sauce while whisking continuously. Continue to cook until the sauce has thickened slightly, approximately 2 to 3 minutes. Remove the pot from the heat and set aside until needed. Remove and discard the star anise pod.

For the chick*n, add the oil to a wok or large skillet over medium-high heat. Lightly brown the chick*n strips in the oil then add the onion, pepper, carrot and broccoli and stir-fry for 4 to 5 minutes until the onions just begin to darken in color. Add the water to the wok and continue stir-frying until all of the water has cooked off, approximately 3 to 4 minutes. You want the veggies to soften but still retain some crunch. If they're too crunchy, add another ¼ cup (60 ml) of water.

Add the teriyaki sauce to the wok and mix everything together with a wooden spoon or spatula. Cook, stirring constantly, for 5 to 6 minutes until the sauce has thickened and sticks to the chick*n and veggies.

Serve with jasmine rice or quinoa.

Szechuan Beef

It seems like no matter how much of our signature Szechuan Beef that we make ... we never make enough.

. . . .

Sauce

½ cup (120 ml) tamari or soy sauce

½ cup (120 ml) water

½ cup (120 g) evaporated cane sugar

¼ cup (15 g) chopped fresh ginger

¼ cup (60 ml) agave syrup

2 tbsp (30 ml) rice vinegar

1 tbsp (15 ml) mirin

1 tbsp (15 g) sambal oelek

Stir Fry

1 Seitan Loaf (page 55) or substitute your favorite vegan beef strips

Grape-seed or canola oil, to shallow fry

Cornstarch, to coat

1 sweet onion, cut in ¼-inch (6-mm) half moons

1 red pepper, cut in ¼-inch (6-mm) strips

¾ cup (125 g) small broccoli florets

Toasted sesame seeds, for garnish

Blend the tamari, water, sugar, ginger, agave, vinegar, mirin and sambal oelek on high, approximately 4 to 5 minutes, until the ginger and sugar have dissolved and the sauce is smooth. Set aside.

Cut the Seitan Loaf into ½ × ½ × 3-inch (13 × 13 × 76-mm) strips.

Add ¼ inch (6 mm) of oil to a wok or large skillet on medium-high heat. Place 2 to 3 tablespoons (18 to 29 g) of cornstarch in a plastic zip bag. Add a few strips of the Seitan Loaf to the bag and shake well to coat. Remove the strips, shaking off any excess cornstarch, and place them in the hot oil using tongs. Do not crowd the wok. Cook, turning the strips every 30 seconds, for a total of 2 minutes or until crispy and golden on all sides. Remove the strips to a paper towel to drain, and repeat with the remaining strips, adding more cornstarch or oil as needed.

Clean the wok, add 2 tablespoons (30 ml) of oil and place it over medium heat. When the oil is hot, add the onions, red pepper and broccoli. Stir fry for 2 to 3 minutes until the veggies have softened. Add the seitan strips to the wok and continue to stir-fry for 2 minutes. Raise the heat to medium-high and add 1 cup (240 ml) of your reserved sauce to the wok. Mix it all together with a wooden spoon so that everything is coated in the sauce. Add additional sauce as needed. At this point, all of the strips should be coated in sauce and there should be a pool of about ¼ cup (60 ml) of the sauce in the bottom of the wok.

Continue to stir-fry, moving everything about, for 2 to 3 minutes or until the sauce has thickened and lovingly coats the seitan strips and veggies.

We like to serve this over jasmine rice or soba noodles sprinkled with toasted sesame seeds. Any remaining sauce lasts for about a week covered in the fridge.

General Tso's Tofu

If you love tofu, you're going to really love this dish! If you hate tofu, you're still going to really love this dish! Our plant-based, no harm/no fowl version of the classic Asian dish General Tso's chicken is the perfect marriage of sweet, spicy and savory. It's loaded with protein, and it's ready in less than 30 minutes from prep to plate.

. . . .

2 (416-g) blocks extra firm tofu (see note)

3 tbsp (45 ml) canola oil, divided

¼ cup (34 g) cornstarch

2 tsp (10 ml) sesame oil

1 small sweet onion, thinly sliced

3 tbsp (45 g) ginger, peeled and finely chopped

1 tsp red chili flakes

Sauce

½ cup (100 g) brown sugar

½ cup (120 ml) water

¼ cup (60 ml) organic ketchup

3 tbsp (45 ml) vegan hoisin sauce

3 tbsp (45 ml) rice vinegar

2 tbsp (30 ml) tamari or soy sauce

Drain and press the tofu. Cut the tofu into ¾-inch (19-mm) cubes. Heat 2 tablespoons (30 ml) of canola oil in a wok or skillet over medium-high heat. Place the cornstarch in a plastic zip bag and add the tofu. Shake until the tofu is coated on all sides with the cornstarch. Remove the tofu and shake off any excess cornstarch.

Add the tofu to the wok in batches (do not overcrowd) and cook for approximately 2 minutes per side until all sides are lightly browned. Remove the tofu and let it drain on paper towel while you repeat the process with the remaining tofu. Add additional oil as required.

To make the sauce, mix the sugar, water, ketchup, hoisin, vinegar and tamari together in a medium bowl and set aside.

Heat 1 tablespoon (15 ml) of canola oil and the sesame oil in a wok or skillet. When the oils are hot, add the onions and sauté until soft and lightly colored, approximately 4 to 5 minutes. Add the ginger and continue to sauté for 2 minutes. Add the chili flakes and continue to sauté for 1 minute. Add the sauce to the wok and cook, stirring constantly, for 3 to 4 minutes or until the sugar dissolves. Add the tofu to the wok. Gently stir until the tofu is coated with sauce. Continue to cook until the sauce thickens, approximately 5 to 6 minutes.

Serve over brown rice or quinoa . . . or you can be like me and eat it straight out of the wok!

Note: Always search out non-GMO tofu for tofu recipes. To press the tofu, wrap the blocks in a double layer of paper towel. Place the wrapped tofu on a cutting board with a plate or sheet pan on top. Weigh down the tofu by placing 2 or 3 cans (cans of tomatoes or beans work great) on top of the plate or sheet pan and let rest for 15 minutes.

Festive Loaf

We whip up this Festive Loaf at Christmas and Thanksgiving, and we regularly sell out!
It takes a little bit of work—but once you find the feel it comes together quite easily.

. . . .

1 cup (240 ml) vegetable stock

4 cups (140 g) multigrain bread cubes

2 tbsp (30 ml) olive oil

1 stalk small diced celery

¼ cup (40 g) small diced sweet onion

½ Granny Smith apple, peeled, cored and diced small

3 tbsp (19 g) dried cranberries

2 tbsp (5 g) minced fresh parsley

½ tsp dried sage

½ tsp dried thyme

¼ cup (30 g) chopped pecans

Almond flour

1 recipe Plant-Based Chick*n (page 69), taken to the resting stage only

Preheat the oven to 400°F (204°C). Warm the vegetable stock in a small pot over low heat.

Place the cubed bread on a parchment paper lined baking sheet and toast in the oven for 4 to 5 minutes until the cubes are crisp and lightly colored. Shake the baking sheet from time to time so that they color evenly.

Heat the olive oil in a large skillet over medium heat. When the oil is hot add the celery, onion, apple and cranberries. Sauté 7 to 9 minutes or until the veggies have softened a bit. Add the parsley, sage, thyme and pecans, and continue to sauté for 5 minutes.

Place the cubed bread in a large bowl and add the sautéed veggie mixture. Stir together. Add ½ cup (120 ml) of the stock and mix everything together with a rubber spatula. The bread will absorb the stock. Continue to add stock until the bread is soft, but not mushy.

Sprinkle a clean countertop and a rolling pin with almond flour and gently roll out the Plant-Based Chick*n to form a rectangle. Be patient—vital wheat gluten is very elastic. Continue to roll the dough, lightly sprinkling with almond flour as needed, until it is ½-inch (13-mm)-thick.

Spoon a thick line of the stuffing down the middle of the rectangle, leaving 2 inches (50 mm) clear all around. You want to load up on the stuffing, but remember that you're going to have to form this into a loaf in a minute, so you don't want to overstuff it.

Gently lift the edge closest to you and roll it over the filling so that you have about 2 inches (50 mm) of overlap with the opposite edge. Pinch together both ends of the loaf and tuck them under the loaf.

Preheat the oven to 350°F (177°C).

Fill a pot large enough to hold the loaf with 2 inches (50 mm) of water and bring the water to a soft boil. Set a steamer basket inside the pot. Loosely wrap the loaf in aluminum foil and place the wrapped loaf in the steamer basket. Cover the pot and let it steam for 20 minutes. Check your water level from time to time to make sure you don't steam the pot dry. Add additional water if necessary.

Remove the loaf and transfer it to a casserole dish. Very carefully remove the aluminum foil. Spoon 3 or 4 tablespoons (45 to 60 ml) of vegetable stock over the loaf and place the casserole dish in the oven for 15 minutes. You want the outside to brown a bit, but watch that the bottom doesn't get too dark.

Slice in thick slices and top the slices with our Shiitake Miso Gravy (page 151).

Carrot Not Dogs

Not Dogs—the quintessential vegan hot dog—are complete with the charred crunchy skin and soft meaty interior. This puppy gives the ballpark frank a serious run for its money. And as a bonus, you can easily pronounce all of the ingredients—something that can't be said for most commercially produced hot dogs!

. . . .

8 carrots, about the size of a hot dog

1 cup (240 ml) water

1 cup (240 ml) tamari or soy sauce

¼ cup (60 ml) rice vinegar

¼ cup (60 ml) canola oil

2 tbsp (30 ml) apple cider vinegar

¼ tsp hickory liquid smoke

4 small cloves garlic, chopped

1 tsp ginger powder

1 tsp coarse grind pepper (sometimes called butcher's grind)

½ tsp onion powder

8 vegan hot dog buns

Wash and gently scrub the carrots. Trim off the tip and tail, but do not peel them. Bring a large pot of salted water to a boil and add the carrots. Cook until the carrots are easily pierced with a skewer, approximately 15 to 17 minutes, depending on the thickness of the carrots.

While the carrots are cooking, prepare the marinade. In a large flat bowl, whisk together the water, tamari, rice vinegar, oil, cider vinegar, liquid smoke, garlic, ginger powder, pepper and onion powder.

When the carrots are ready, remove them from the boiling water and place them in the marinade. Make certain that all of the carrots are coated with the marinade, cover the bowl and refrigerate for a minimum of 4 hours. If you plan in advance, marinating the carrots overnight is even better.

Fire up the grill! Once the grill is hot, remove the carrots from the marinade and place them on the grill. Grill the carrots for 45 to 60 seconds until they are nicely grill marked and slightly charred. Turn the carrots one-quarter turn and repeat until all sides are grill marked.

Lightly toast the hot dog buns on the grill, add a Not Dog and dress it with the condiments of your choice.

You can top these Not Dogs with the usual suspects: mustard, relish, ketchup, pickle and sauerkraut, or give them a try loaded with our 3C Slaw (page 128). It's a match made in Not Dog heaven.

Ground Beet Burger

Makes 6 to 8 Burgers

We've featured this burger in our butcher counter since opening YamChops in June of 2012, and it's been a struggle to keep it in stock since day one! It's a bit of work, but I promise you . . . it's worth every second. These burgers can also be frozen, which, when loosely translated, means—double up!

· ·

1 tbsp (15 ml) grape-seed or canola oil

1 cup (150 g) diced sweet onion

3 cloves garlic, minced

1 cup (210 g) peeled and grated white potato

1 cup (50 g) peeled and grated carrot

1 cup (150 g) peeled and grated red beet

1 cup (250 g) trimmed and grated zucchini

1 cup (195 g) cooked brown rice

2 tbsp (5 g) chopped fresh parsley

1 tbsp (3 g) chopped fresh dill

1 tbsp (3 g) chopped fresh tarragon

½ cup (50 g) chopped walnuts

1 cup (320 g) cooked and mashed potatoes (we use Yukon Gold)

2 tbsp (30 ml) tamari or soy sauce

1½ tbsp (5 g) nutritional yeast

¼ tsp sea salt

⅛ tsp freshly ground black pepper

Preheat the oven to 350°F (177°C).

Heat the oil in a medium skillet over medium heat. Add the onion and sauté until translucent, approximately 5 minutes. Add the garlic and continue to sauté for 2 more minutes. Remove the mixture from the heat and allow it to cool.

Place all of the grated vegetables in a strainer, and let them rest for 30 minutes to drain off any excess water.

Once the onion mixture has cooled, add it to a processor along with the rice, parsley, dill, tarragon and walnuts. Pulse the mixture 5 or 6 times until it is coarsely blended.

Empty the mixture from the processor into a large bowl and add the drained vegetables, mashed potatoes, tamari, nutritional yeast, salt and pepper.

With your hands, mix everything together in the bowl until it is fully integrated. You may want to don a pair of plastic gloves as the beet will color the mixture (and your hands) red.

Form the burgers, place them on a parchment paper lined baking sheet and refrigerate for 15 minutes. At YamChops we use a 4 ounce (115 g) scoop to measure our burgers. You want the formed burgers to be approximately ½-inch (13-mm) thick.

Bake the burgers for 30 minutes, carefully flipping them over halfway through the cooking time. The burgers will firm up in the oven.

To finish the burgers, place the baked burgers on a preheated grill and grill them until they are nicely marked on both sides, approximately 45 seconds per side.

Grab yourself some fresh burger buns and the toppings of your choice. We'd highly recommend topping these burgers with spicy mustard and our 3C Slaw (page 128).

YamBurger

It just goes without saying that YamChops, North America's first plant-based butcher shop, would feature a YamBurger.

4 tbsp (60 ml) olive oil, divided

¾ cup (115 g) diced sweet onion

2 cups (370 g) white beans, rinsed and drained

2 cups (450 g) peeled and grated yam or sweet potato

½ cup (23 g) nutritional yeast

¼ cup (55 g) chopped kale or spinach

¼ cup (60 g) tahini

1½ tsp (7 ml) cider vinegar

1 tsp garlic powder

¾ tsp chipotle powder

½ tsp sea salt

¼ tsp coarse grind pepper (sometimes called butcher's grind)

¾ cup (140 g) cooked quinoa

¾ cup (68 g) rolled oats, finely pulsed in a processor

Heat 2 tablespoons (30 ml) of olive oil in a skillet over medium heat and sauté the onions until softened, approximately 7 to 8 minutes. Remove from the heat and set aside to cool.

Coarsely mash the white beans in a bowl. You want to leave a bit of texture in the beans.

Add the beans, yams, nutritional yeast, kale, tahini, vinegar, garlic powder, chipotle powder, salt, pepper and quinoa to a large bowl. Mix well with your hands until all of the ingredients are fully combined.

Mix in the oat flour, a couple of spoonfuls at a time, until the mixture just holds together. Form the mixture into burgers and place them on a parchment lined baking sheet. You want the formed burgers to be approximately ½-inch (13-mm) thick. The burgers will be quite soft at this stage. Place the burgers in your freezer for 20 minutes or in your refrigerator for 2 hours to set up.

Preheat the oven to 350°F (177 °C).

Set a large frying pan over medium-high heat and add 2 tablespoons (30 ml) of olive oil. When the oil is hot, add 3 or 4 of the burgers to the pan. Do not crowd them.

You're out to form a golden crust on the burgers. The crust helps to hold the burgers together. The best way to do this is to cook the burgers undisturbed for 3 to 4 minutes, gently flip them, and cook them for 3 to 4 minutes on the second side. Remove the burgers to a parchment paper lined baking sheet, and place the sheet in the oven for 10 to 12 minutes or until the burgers are heated through.

Load them up with your favorite condiments or try them topped with our Asian Pear, Daikon and Carrot Slaw (page 129). YamGood!

Grilled Indonesian-Style Tofu Steaks with Roasted Cashew and Mango Salsa

These tofu steaks pack a whole lotta flavor and a ton of protein. Topped off with our roasted cashew and mango salsa, these steaks make an excellent appetizer served hot or at room temperature.

• •

2 (416-g) blocks extra firm tofu, pressed (see note)

2 tbsp (30 ml) grape-seed or vegetable oil

1 tbsp (8 g) ground ginger

1 tbsp (8 g) ground coriander

1½ tsp (5 g) turmeric powder

1½ tsp (5 g) garlic powder

1 tbsp (15 g) sambal oelek

1 tbsp (9 g) brown sugar

1 tsp sea salt

Roasted Cashew and Mango Salsa

2 ripe, but firm, mangos, peeled and diced small

1 roasted red pepper, diced small

½ cup (75 g) chopped roasted cashews (unsalted)

⅓ cup (17 g) thinly sliced green onions

3 tbsp (8 g) chopped fresh basil

2 tbsp (30 ml) lime juice

1 tbsp (3 g) chopped fresh mint

1 tbsp (13 g) minced jalapeño

Working from the short side of the tofu block, cut the tofu into ½-inch (13-mm) planks. Spread the planks on paper towel to drain while you prepare the paste.

Heat the oil in a small pot over low heat for 5 minutes. When the oil is heated through, remove the pot from the burner and whisk in the ginger, coriander, turmeric and garlic powder.

Mix the sambal oelek, brown sugar and salt together in a small bowl. Add the mixture to the pot and whisk together very well to form a paste.

Heat up a grill pan or countertop griller to high.

Coat the tofu planks with the paste. The best way to do this is to spread the paste over the tofu with your hands (wearing plastic gloves). Lay the tofu planks on the grill and grill them until they are nicely grill marked, approximately 30 to 45 seconds per side. Turn the planks 45 degrees to form an eye-catching diamond pattern with the grill marks.

Combine all of the salsa ingredients in a bowl and mix together.

Remove the planks to a serving platter and top with a heaping spoonful of roasted cashew and mango salsa.

Note: Always search out non-GMO tofu for tofu recipes. To press the tofu, wrap the blocks in a double layer of paper towels. Place the wrapped tofu on a cutting board with a plate or sheet pan on top. Weigh down the tofu by placing 2 or 3 cans (cans of tomatoes or beans work great) on top of the plate or sheet pan and let rest for 15 minutes.

Thai Tofu Burgers

This kicked-up burger was created for a workshop I did at Veg Food Fest in Toronto, North America's largest vegan festival. It's a three day vegan extravaganza featuring tons of food vendors and everything else associated with living a vegan life. We love these tangy bundles of flavor served with or without a bun and topped with our Asian Pear, Daikon and Carrot Slaw (page 129).

Makes 6 to 8 Burgers

1 (416-g) block extra firm tofu (see note)

2 tbsp (30 ml) egg replacer mixed with 6 tbsp (88 ml) warm water

½ cup (75 g) roasted chopped cashews (unsalted)

1 cup (185 g) cooked quinoa

½ cup (25 g) panko

½ cup (25 g) chopped green onion

½ cup (50 g) grated carrot

3 tbsp (45 g) Thai red curry paste

2 tbsp (5 g) chopped fresh basil

2 tsp (10 ml) Sriracha

2 tsp (4 g) lime zest

1 tbsp (15 ml) canola oil

Note: Always search out non-GMO tofu for tofu recipes. To press tofu, wrap the blocks in a double layer of paper towels. Place the wrapped tofu on a cutting board with a plate or sheet pan on top. Weigh down the tofu by placing 2 or 3 cans (cans of tomatoes or beans work great) on top of the plate or sheet pan and let rest for 15 minutes.

Drain and press the tofu for 15 minutes. Prepare the egg replacer by whisking it with water in a small bowl. Set the mixture aside to rest until needed. Pulse the cashews 3 or 4 times in the food processor. You're after a medium-fine texture.

Grate the tofu on the large holes of a box grater, or crumble it by hand into a large bowl. Add the cashews, quinoa, panko, green onion and carrot, and mix together well.

Combine the curry paste, basil, Sriracha, lime zest and egg replacer mixture in a small processor and pulse until fully blended together. Add this mixture to the tofu mixture, and with your hands, gently fold the ingredients together until they are fully combined. Cover the bowl with plastic wrap and refrigerate for 1 hour. Or, if you're a really good planner, make this mixture the day before you need it and let it refrigerate overnight.

Preheat the oven to 350°F (177°C).

Remove the burger mixture from the fridge and form the burgers. At YamChops, we gently press these burgers in 4-inch (100-mm) patty molds or 2-inch (50-mm) slider molds. You can make them any size you'd like, but just remember to make them at least ½- to ¾-inch (13- to 19-mm)-thick. That said, keep in mind that this is a pretty soft burger before you crisp it, and flipping soft burgers gets harder the bigger they are.

Heat the canola oil in a large frying pan over medium heat. When hot, carefully lower 3 or 4 burgers into the pan. Remember, leave some room to flip! Cook for 3 to 4 minutes or until the bottom is crispy—because crispy is good, and it also serves to hold these burgers together. Gently flip them over and cook until the second side is crispy, approximately 3 to 4 minutes. When done, place the burgers on a parchment paper lined sheet pan. Repeat with the remaining burgers, adding additional oil as necessary.

Place the sheet pan in the oven and cook the burgers for 12 minutes or until they are heated through.

Samosa Burger

This burger was inspired by the classic East Indian samosa—packed with veggies and boldly spiced. Give these patties a try topped with our Mango Tamarind Chutney (page 154).

. . . .

3 cups (675 g) Yukon Gold potato, cut into ¾-inch (19-mm) cubes

1½ cups (345 g) small cauliflower florets

1 cup (175 g) fresh or frozen corn kernels, thawed if using frozen

¾ cup (115 g) fresh or frozen peas, thawed if using frozen

3 tbsp (10 g) chopped green onions

2 tbsp (5 g) minced fresh basil

2 tbsp (18 g) mild curry powder

1 tbsp (9 g) garam masala

1 tbsp (9 g) onion powder

1 tsp coarse grind pepper (sometimes called butcher's grind)

½ tsp sea salt

¼ tsp turmeric powder

¼ tsp cayenne pepper

2 cups (200 g) coarsely ground raw cashews, divided

Sliced red onion

Cherry tomatoes, halved

Preheat the oven to 400°F (204°C). Lightly spray a parchment lined baking sheet with canola oil spray.

Bring a pot of salted water to a boil over high heat. Once boiling, add the potato cubes and cook for 8 to 9 minutes or until they can be easily pierced with a skewer. Drain the potatoes in a colander and run them under cold water to halt the cooking process, and drain them again. Put the drained potatoes in a large bowl and roughly mash them with a fork. You want to keep some chunks in the mash.

Pulse the cauliflower florets in a food processor a few times until they are about the size of corn kernels. Add the cauliflower, corn, peas, green onions and basil to the potatoes and fold everything together using a spatula.

Mix the curry powder, garam masala, onion powder, pepper, salt, turmeric and cayenne pepper together in a small bowl. Sprinkle the spice mix over the potato mixture, and mix everything together with a spatula.

Add half of the cashews to the potato mixture and mix together well. Continue to add the cashews until the mixture begins to bind. Using a ⅓ or ½ cup (80 to 120 ml) measure, shape the mixture into patties approximately ½-inch (13-mm) thick. Place the burgers on the prepared baking sheet and spray them lightly with canola oil spray. Place the patties in the oven for 12 minutes, flip them and place them back in the oven for 8 additional minutes, or until the burgers are golden and have firmed up.

Serve them topped with Mango Tamarind Chutney (page 154), sliced red onion and tomatoes.

Korean BBQ Ribs

These finger lickin' ribs feature our Korean BBQ Sauce. It starts out sweet then turns on the heat! This sauce takes burgers, grilled chick*n, baked portobello mushrooms, roasted potatoes and tacos to new heights. For a more traditional rib, substitute your favorite BBQ sauce in place of the Korean BBQ Sauce.

· ·

Sauce

½ cup (135 g) Korean red chili paste (gochujang)

⅓ cup (50 g) evaporated cane sugar

¼ cup (60 ml) water

2 tbsp (30 ml) tamari or soy sauce

2 tbsp (30 ml) rice vinegar

2 tsp (10 ml) sesame oil

2 tsp (6 g) minced garlic

2 tsp (10 g) minced ginger

Ribs

1¾ cups + 2 tbsp (233 g) vital wheat gluten

1 cup (90 g) chickpea flour, plus more for dusting

1 tbsp (3 g) nutritional yeast

1 tbsp (7 g) Spanish paprika

1 tbsp (8 g) onion powder

1½ tsp (4 g) garlic powder

1½ cups (360 ml) vegetable stock

¼ cup + 1 tbsp (75 g) tahini

2 tbsp (30 ml) tamari or soy sauce

2 tsp (10 ml) hickory liquid smoke

Preheat the oven to 350°F (177°C).

To prepare the sauce, whisk the chili paste, sugar, water, tamari, vinegar, oil, garlic and ginger together in a pot over medium-low heat. Let it simmer for 20 to 25 minutes, whisking from time to time until it thickens and is the consistency of BBQ sauce. Once thickened, set the sauce aside.

To prepare the ribs, combine the vital wheat gluten, chickpea flour, nutritional yeast, paprika, onion powder and garlic powder in the bowl of a stand mixer fitted with a dough hook. Mix on low speed for 4 minutes. Whisk together the stock, tahini, tamari and liquid smoke in a bowl. Add it to the mixer and continue to mix on low speed for 6 minutes. Turn the dough out onto a countertop dusted with chickpea flour. Knead the dough, adding additional chickpea flour as necessary so that the dough does not stick to your fingers or your countertop.

Let the dough rest on the counter covered with a clean towel for 30 minutes.

Cut the dough into 4 pieces and stretch each piece into a rack of ribs shape no thicker than ½ inch (13 mm). If the dough is too elastic and doesn't maintain its shape, knead in another tablespoon or two (6 or 12 g) of chickpea flour.

Preheat the grill, grill pan or countertop griller.

Place the 4 racks of ribs on a parchment lined baking sheet and place them in the oven for 15 minutes. Remove and brush both sides generously with Korean BBQ sauce. Return to the oven for an additional 15 minutes. Remove from the oven and brush both sides once again with the Korean BBQ sauce.

Place the racks on the grill and cook for 2 to 3 minutes per side, or until the racks are nicely grill marked. Turn the racks 45 degrees halfway through the cooking time to make those really nice diamond-shaped grill marks.

Place the racks on your cutting board and brush them one last time with the Korean BBQ sauce. Cut the racks width wise into 1-inch (25-mm) ribs.

Serve with additional Korean BBQ sauce on the side.

No-Crab Crab Cakes

This veganization of crab cakes came about when I was stopped by a mesmerizing photo in an Asian cookbook. It was definitely a drool-worthy pic! The mission to replicate that dish began, and here's the result.

. . . .

Lemongrass Cream

1 cup (240 ml) Cashew Sour Cream (page 140)

2 stalks lemongrass, cut into 2-inch (50-mm) pieces and smashed

1-inch (25-mm) piece of ginger, peeled and smashed

4 large cloves garlic, peeled and smashed

Crab Cakes

1 (416-g) block extra firm tofu, drained and pressed (see notes)

1 tbsp (15 ml) vegan fish sauce (nuoc mam chay, see notes)

½ tbsp (8 ml) tamari or soy sauce

1 cup (225 g) diced celery

1 cup (125 g) diced water chestnuts, drained

½ cup (75 g) diced red onion

½ cup (90 g) diced red pepper

½ cup (15 g) chopped fresh parsley

1 tbsp (15 g) minced ginger

1 tbsp (15 g) finely minced lemongrass, inner white part of the stalk only

2 tbsp (30 ml) egg replacer mixed with 6 tbsp (89 ml) warm water

1 to 1½ cups (50 to 75 g) panko, plus more for breading

Grape-seed or canola oil, for shallow frying

Prepare the lemongrass cream by heating the Cashew Sour Cream, lemongrass, ginger and garlic in a pot over medium heat. Cook, stirring regularly, for 5 to 7 minutes until the cream just begins to bubble. Turn down the heat to low and simmer the cream, stirring regularly, for 20 minutes or until the volume in the pot has been reduced by one-half. Strain the flavored cream into a bowl and set it in the fridge to cool down a bit.

Shred the tofu into a large bowl, using the large holes of a grater. Add the vegan fish sauce and tamari and stir with a spatula to combine.

Add the celery, water chestnuts, red onion, red pepper and parsley to the tofu and fold it all together to evenly distribute the veggies. Add the cooled and strained flavored cream to the tofu mixture along with the ginger and lemongrass and mix gently with a spatula.

Whisk the egg replacer with the water in a small bowl until it's smooth. Add it to the tofu mixture and fold everything together.

Add 1 cup (50 g) of panko and, with your hands, gently mix it into the tofu. Add additional panko as necessary until the mixture binds together.

Form the tofu into cakes and lightly coat the outside with the remaining panko. Place the cakes in the refrigerator for a minimum of 4 hours for them to set up.

Preheat the oven to 225°F (107°C).

Heat ½ inch (13 mm) of oil in a large skillet over medium-high heat. When hot, shallow fry the cakes for 2 to 3 minutes per side until they are golden. Do not crowd the pan. Drain the cakes on a paper towel and place them on a parchment paper lined baking sheet. Place the baking sheet in the oven until you're ready to serve, but for no more than 30 minutes or the cakes will start to dry out.

We love these beauties topped with some Sriracha Aioli (page 147).

Notes: Always search out non-GMO tofu for tofu recipes. To press the tofu, wrap the blocks in a double layer of paper towels. Place the wrapped tofu on a cutting board with a plate or sheet pan on top. Weigh down the tofu by placing 2 or 3 cans (cans of tomatoes or beans work great) on top of the plate or sheet pan and let rest for 15 minutes.

If you can't find nuoc mam chay, you can substitute 1½ teaspoons (7 ml) soy sauce and 1½ teaspoons (7 ml) fresh lime juice.

Beer-Battered Hearts of Palm Fysh Sticks

You had us at beer battered! Who'd've thought that hearts of palm would make the perfect fysh stick? Moist and flaky on the inside, perfectly crunchy on the outside. Top them with vegan tartar sauce and serve with a batch of roasted Yukon Gold potatoes for an old time fysh fry!

· ·

1 cup (125 g) unbleached all-purpose or gluten-free flour, divided

¼ cup (34 g) cornstarch

2 tsp (7 g) baking powder

¾ tsp sea salt

½ tsp Old Bay seasoning

1 cup (240 ml) vegan dark beer

2 (14-oz [397-g]) cans whole hearts of palm

Grape-seed or canola oil, for frying

Mix ¾ cup (94 g) flour, cornstarch, baking powder, salt and Old Bay seasoning together in a large bowl. Slowly add the beer while whisking gently. Mix until the batter is just smooth—some small lumps are okay. Set aside to rest for 20 minutes.

Preheat the oven to 250°F (121°C).

Drain and rinse the hearts of palm. Slice each whole heart of palm from top to bottom on the diagonal so you end up with two long rounded triangles.

Once the batter has rested, set a skillet over medium heat and add ½ inch (13 mm) of oil. Drop a droplet of the batter into the hot oil. If it turns golden in 30 seconds, you're good to go.

Working in batches, dust two hearts of palm with the remaining flour and submerge them in the batter. Carefully lift them out and let the excess batter drip off for 10 seconds. Gently lower the battered hearts of palm into the oil. Cook for 1 to 2 minutes until the bottom is golden, then gently turn and cook for 1 to 2 minutes until the second side is golden.

Remove to a paper towel lined plate to drain. Place in the oven to keep warm while you cook the remaining fysh sticks.

Note: The fysh can be prepared up to 4 hours in advance. Prepare the recipe. Cover the paper towel lined plate of cooked fysh with plastic wrap and place it in the refrigerator. When ready to reheat, gently place the fysh on a parchment lined sheet pan and place it in a preheated 350°F (177°C) oven for 8 to 10 minutes or until heated through and crispy. The fysh will be quite soft when you remove them from the refrigerator but they will crisp up nicely in the oven.

Root Beer–Battered Tofish

Created while in England working toward one of my plant-based cooking degrees, this quintessentially British mainstay (with a whimsical Canadian twist) is everything you're looking for from this classic dish—except the fish part, of course. Don't forget the chips and the cider vinegar and the tartar sauce and the ketchup and the wasabi mayo . . .

. . . .

1 cup (125 g) unbleached all-purpose or gluten-free flour, divided

¼ cup (34 g) cornstarch

2 tsp (8 g) baking powder

¾ tsp sea salt

½ tsp Old Bay seasoning

1 cup (240 ml) organic root beer

2 (416-g) blocks extra firm tofu (see note)

3 or 4 sheets sushi nori

Grape-seed or canola oil, for frying

Note: Always search out non-GMO tofu for all tofu recipes. To press the tofu, wrap the blocks in a double layer of paper towels. Place the wrapped tofu on a cutting board with a plate or sheet pan on top. Weigh down the tofu by placing 2 or 3 cans (cans of tomatoes or beans work great) on top of the plate or sheet pan and let rest for 15 minutes.

Mix ¾ cup (94 g) of flour, cornstarch, baking powder, salt and Old Bay seasoning together in a large bowl. Slowly add the root beer while whisking gently. Mix until the batter is just smooth—some small lumps are okay. Set aside to rest for 20 minutes.

Drain and press the tofu.

Preheat the oven to 250°F (120°C).

Remove the tofu blocks—lay them on their side—and cut them in half vertically to form two ½- to ¾-inch (13- to 19-mm)-thick planks. Then cut each plank in half to give you 4 fillets per tofu block.

Cut the nori sheet to fit each fillet and press it onto 1 side of each fillet.

Once the batter has rested, set a skillet over medium heat and add ½ inch (13 mm) of oil. Drop a droplet of the batter into the hot oil. If it turns golden in 30 seconds, you're good to go.

Working in batches, dust two fillets with some of the remaining flour and submerge them in the batter. Carefully lift them out and let the excess batter drip off for 10 seconds. Gently lower the battered fillets, nori side up, into the frying pan. Cook until the bottom is golden, then gently turn and cook until the second side is golden.

Remove to a paper towel–lined plate to drain. Place in the oven to keep warm while you cook the remaining tofish.

The tofish can be prepared up to 4 hours in advance. Prepare the complete recipe and cover the paper towel–lined plate of tofish with plastic wrap and place in the refrigerator. When ready to reheat, gently place the tofish on a parchment paper lined sheet pan and place in a preheated 350°F (177°C) oven for 8 to 10 minutes until heated through and crispy. The tofish will be quite soft when you remove them from the refrigerator but they will crisp up nicely in the oven.

Fishless Tacos

Tacos, for me, are kinda like a feast in your fist!

Whip up a batch of Fysh Sticks (page 41) or Tofish (page 42) and turn them into this handful of flavor.

. . . .

Purple Cabbage Slaw

2 cups (200 g) purple cabbage, shredded

2 tbsp (30 ml) lime juice

1 tbsp (15 ml) agave syrup

¼ tsp sea salt

Mango Salsa

2 mangos, peeled and diced small

3 tbsp (25 g) minced red onion

2 tbsp (5 g) minced fresh basil

1 tbsp (15 ml) agave syrup

1 tbsp (15 ml) lime juice

⅛ tsp sea salt

Taco Sauce

1 cup (220 g) vegan mayo

2 tbsp (30 ml) lime juice

2 tbsp (25 g) minced jalapeño pepper (leave seeds in if you like things spicier)

2 tbsp (30 ml) coconut milk

1 tbsp (5 g) capers, rinsed well (chop if you use large capers)

1 tbsp (3 g) minced fresh basil

1 tsp ground cumin

½ tsp chipotle chili powder

½ tsp Mexican chili powder

½ tsp dried dill

½ tsp dried oregano

8 corn or whole wheat soft taco shells

Fysh (page 41) or Tofish (page 42)

Mix the cabbage, lime juice, agave and salt for the cabbage slaw together in a bowl. Cover the bowl and refrigerate until needed.

Mix the mango, onion, basil, agave, lime juice and salt together for the salsa in a bowl. Cover the bowl and refrigerate until needed.

Whisk the mayo, lime juice, jalapeño, coconut milk, capers, basil, cumin, chili powders, dill and oregano for the taco sauce together in a bowl. Cover the bowl and refrigerate until needed.

Warm the taco shells for 3 minutes in a 350° F (177° C) oven or for 12 seconds in a microwave set to high.

Layer the taco shells with purple cabbage slaw, Fysh or Tofish (sliced), mango salsa and taco sauce, and then open wide!

Butternut Squash Steak

This dish regularly takes center stage at our Thanksgiving or Christmas table. If you follow a plant-based diet, you've probably seen, but have never used, Montreal steak seasoning. Well that ends today! Couple these beauties, featuring Montreal steak seasoning, with mashed potatoes and Shiitake Miso Gravy (page 151) for a festive meal any day of the year.

· ·

2–3 butternut squash necks (see note)

Olive oil

Montreal steak seasoning

Preheat the oven to 350°F (177°C), and preheat a grill pan or countertop griller.

Cut the necks of the butternut squash from the base and trim off the stem ends. Peel the butternut squash and, very carefully, with a very sharp knife, slice the necks into ½-inch (13-mm)-thick planks. You want to count two steaks per person, thus the number of squash you will need will depend on how many steaks you can get from the squash. What I'm trying to say is, look for squash with big necks!

When the grill pan is hot, brush both sides of the squash planks with the olive oil. Grill the squash steaks for 4 to 5 minutes per side until they are nicely marked. Turn the steaks 45 degrees to form an eye-catching diamond pattern with the grill marks. Place the grilled steaks on the cutting board. Brush them once again with the olive oil and generously coat both sides with the Montreal steak seasoning. Place them on a parchment paper lined baking sheet and bake for approximately 20 minutes or until they are easily pierced with a skewer.

Kick these up a notch and serve them topped with a tablespoon (15 g) of Parsley-Mint Chimichurri (page 153).

Note: Hang on to the base of the squash and whip up a batch of Roasted Butternut Squash Hummus (page 127).

Butternut Squash Cheeze 'n' Mac Casserole

We know that a great mac and cheese is all about the sauce. Our Butternut Squash Cheeze transforms this casserole into a bowl of rich and creamy deliciousness. Comfort food at its best, 'nuf said!

. . . .

1 recipe Butternut Squash Cheeze Sauce (page 146)

1½ lb (680 g) mini pasta shells or elbow macaroni

1 cup (64 g) green kale or spinach, stems removed and cut in ¼-inch (6-mm) strips

1 tbsp (15 ml) olive oil

1 cup (50 g) panko

2 small cloves garlic, minced

Prepare the Butternut Squash Cheeze Sauce.

Cook the pasta according to the package directions. During the last minute of cooking, add the kale strips to the pot with the pasta.

While the pasta is cooking, heat the olive oil in a medium saucepan over medium-low heat. Add the panko and garlic and cook, stirring regularly, until the bread crumbs darken a bit in color, approximately 4 to 5 minutes. Set aside until needed.

When the pasta is al dente, drain it well and return it to the pot. Add the cheeze sauce until you reach your particular level of creaminess and mix well with a wooden spoon. Leftover cheeze sauce can be refrigerated for up to 2 weeks.

Spoon the cheezy pasta into ramekins or bowls and sprinkle generously with the panko.

Serve immediately or keep warm in a 225°F (107°C) oven for up to 30 minutes.

Coconut Peanut Curry

Sometimes, to get through winter up here in The Great White North, we need something that warms us from the inside out! This curry does just that. It's thick, rich and delightfully spiced. Serve this wonderful curry over brown or jasmine rice.

. . . .

2 tbsp (30 ml) grape-seed or canola oil

½ cup (75 g) diced sweet onion

4 small cloves garlic, minced

1 tbsp (15 g) minced ginger

½ cup (90 g) peanut butter

2 tsp (10 g) Thai red curry paste

2 tsp (6 g) turmeric powder

1 tsp ground cumin

1½ cups (350 ml) water

1 (14-oz [400-ml]) can coconut milk

2 tbsp (18 g) brown sugar

2 tsp (10 g) sea salt

1 (416-g) block extra firm tofu (see note)

1 cup (133 g) cubed sweet potato

1 handful green kale (or spinach)

1½ tbsp (22 ml) lime juice

½ cup (75 g) roasted unsalted cashews

Heat the oil over medium heat in a Dutch oven or soup pot. When the oil is hot, add the onions, garlic and ginger. Sauté until soft, approximately 4 to 5 minutes.

Reduce the heat to low and stir in the peanut butter, curry paste, turmeric and cumin. Stir until the peanut butter has melted and the mixture is very fragrant. Whisk in the water, coconut milk, sugar and salt.

Cut the tofu into ½-inch (13-mm) cubes and add to the pot along with the sweet potato cubes. Tear the kale into bite-size pieces and add to the pot. Mix well and let the curry simmer until the sweet potatoes are tender, approximately 30 minutes. Stir the curry regularly.

When ready, remove the curry from the heat and stir in the lime juice and cashews.

Note: Always search out non-GMO tofu for tofu recipes.

Raw Pad Thai

Grab that spiralizer from the back of your cupboard! Our fresh take on Pad Thai tops raw veggie noodles with a delightful ginger-almond dressing. This dressing also makes a great dip.

• •

Ginger-Almond Dressing

½ cup (125 g) almond butter

12 pitted dates

2 tbsp (30 g) tamarind paste

2 tbsp (20 g) chopped jalapeño

1 tbsp (15 g) chopped ginger

3 small cloves garlic

1 tsp sea salt

¾ cup (180 ml) water, divided

Pad Thai Bowls

3 medium carrots, peeled

2 medium green zucchini, ends trimmed

2 medium red beets, peeled

¼ cup (35 g) raw sunflower seeds

¼ cup (37 g) raw sesame seeds

1 tbsp (3 g) nutritional yeast

1 tsp ground cumin

¾ tsp Mexican chili powder

¾ tsp onion powder

To make the ginger-almond dressing, place the almond butter, dates, tamarind paste, jalapeño, ginger, garlic, salt and ½ cup (120 ml) of water in a high-speed blender. Blend on high until smooth, adding the remaining ¼ cup (60 ml) of water as necessary to reach a thick, but pourable, consistency.

Spiralize the carrots, zucchini and beets, and keep them in separate stacks. Place a small stack of each veggie on each serving plate. By the way, if you don't have a spiralizer, you can grate the beets and the carrots, and you can cut the zucchini in long, thin slices. However, a spiralizer is a whole lotta fun and the noodles make this dish more pad thai-ish.

To make the seed and nut blend, toast the sunflower seeds in a dry frying pan over medium-low heat, shaking the pan very regularly, until the seeds are golden. This should take 6 to 7 minutes, but keep an eye on them. They can go from beautiful to burned in seconds. Remove from the heat and place in a medium bowl.

Wipe the pan and toast the sesame seeds over medium-low heat, shaking the pan very regularly for 4 to 5 minutes, until the seeds are golden. Remove from the heat and place in the bowl with the sunflower seeds.

Add the nutritional yeast, cumin, chili powder and onion powder to the bowl and mix together.

Drizzle each plate with 2 to 3 tablespoons (30 to 45 ml) of the ginger-almond dressing and a generous sprinkling of the seed and nut blend.

Pinto Bean Cutlet

These protein-packed cutlets are best served with a heaping side of mashed potatoes and a generous ladle of chunky mushroom gravy.

. . . .

1½ cups (350 g) canned pinto beans

2 tbsp (30 ml) olive oil, divided

1 tbsp (12 g) almond butter or tahini

½ cup (76 g) vital wheat gluten

½ cup (60 g) bread crumbs

½ cup (120 ml) vegetable stock

3 tbsp (45 ml) tamari or soy sauce

1 tsp apple cider vinegar

2 tsp (5 g) Hungarian paprika

1 tsp garlic powder

¾ tsp dried thyme leaves

¾ tsp dried rosemary leaves

Rinse the pinto beans and drain them well. Add the pinto beans to a food processor and pulse 3 or 4 times. Add 1 tablespoon (15 ml) of the olive oil and almond butter and pulse in 4-second spurts until the pinto beans are coarsely mashed. You want to keep some of the texture of the pinto beans, but you don't want pieces that are bigger than a whole peppercorn. You are not going for a smooth hummus consistency. Be sure to scrape down the sides of the processor and mix the contents with a spatula a couple of times during the process.

Empty the pinto bean mixture into the bowl of your stand mixer fitted with the paddle attachment. Add all of the remaining ingredients except the oil to the bowl and mix on low speed for 5 minutes. Remove the mixture to a clean countertop and knead with your hands for an additional 3 minutes. The mixture should be slightly wet, but not at all sticky. If it's too wet, knead in an additional 1 to 2 teaspoons (2.5 to 5 g) of bread crumbs. If it's too dry, knead in an additional 1 to 2 teaspoons (5 to 10 ml) of stock.

Tear off a piece of dough and roll it into a ball. With both thumbs on top of the ball gently pull the dough apart in opposite directions. If the dough has a fibrous texture when you pull it apart, you're good to go. If it does not, knead it for another 3 or 4 minutes.

Let the dough rest, lightly covered with a clean towel, for 30 minutes on your countertop.

Once the dough has rested, measure off 2½- to 3½-ounce (80- to 100-g) pieces. Press them flat on a lightly floured countertop and, using a rolling pin, gently roll them to approximately ¼-inch (6-mm)-thick cutlets.

Preheat the oven to 350°F (177°C).

Heat the remaining tablespoon (15 ml) of oil in a skillet over medium heat. When the oil is hot, add the pinto bean cutlets and cook for 5 minutes per side or until lightly browned. Place the cutlets on a parchment paper lined baking sheet and place the baking sheet in the oven for 18 minutes, flipping them halfway through the cooking time. You're after cutlets that are firmed up (not hard) and are browned on both sides.

Seitan Loaf

This loaf forms the base for many of our plant-based "meat" recipes. You can slice the loaf deli style for a sandwich or cut it into strips for our Szechuan Beef (page 20) or cut it into cubes for a stir fry or smother it in BBQ sauce and hit the grill.

. . . .

1¼ cups (180 g) vital wheat gluten

3 tbsp (9 g) nutritional yeast

1½ tbsp (9 g) almond flour (see note), plus more for dusting

1 tsp Hungarian paprika

½ tsp Spanish paprika

½ tsp onion powder

¼ tsp garlic powder

½ cup (120 ml) vegetable stock

1½ tbsp + ⅓ cup (102 ml) tamari or soy sauce

1½ tbsp (22 g) tomato paste

1 tbsp (15 g) tahini paste

1 tbsp (15 ml) olive oil

2½ cups (600 ml) vegetable stock

1 cup (240 ml) water

Preheat the oven to 350°F (177°C).

Combine the vital wheat gluten, nutritional yeast, almond flour, paprikas, onion powder and garlic powder in a large bowl and mix well. In a medium bowl, whisk together the vegetable stock, 1½ tablespoons (22 ml) of tamari, tomato paste, tahini and olive oil. Form a well in the dry mixture and add the wet mixture. Using a fork, slowly incorporate the wet mixture into the dry. Once the mixtures are almost fully incorporated, abandon the fork and use your hands. Knead the mixture in the bowl for 2 minutes, incorporating any of the remaining dry mixture from the sides and the bottom of the bowl.

Lightly dust the countertop with almond flour and knead the dough for 5 minutes. Alternatively, you can place the dough in the bowl of a stand mixer fitted with a dough hook. The dough should be a bit damp, but should not stick to your fingers. If it is sticking to your fingers, add 1 to 2 teaspoons (2.5 to 5 g) of almond flour. Shape the dough into a loaf, cover it with a clean towel and let it rest on the counter for 30 minutes.

Combine the stock, water and ⅓ cup (80 ml) of tamari in a pot large enough to hold the seitan loaf and bring them to a boil. Once the broth begins to boil, turn the heat down to simmer. You're after just a gentle simmer—from this point forward you do not want the broth to boil. Add the seitan loaf and simmer it for 1 hour. Gently flip the loaf every 15 minutes.

Remove the loaf from the pot and let it cool to room temperature.

Note: You can make your own almond flour. Place 1 cup (170 g) of raw almonds in a food processor or blender. Pulse in 15-second spurts to grind the almonds into a powder. Be careful not to go beyond the powder stage or you'll end up with almond butter. All things considered, that's not such a bad thing—but for this recipe you're just going for a flour.

Black Bean Meatless Meatballs

Makes 2 Dozen (2 ounce [57 g]) Meatballs

This is our go-to meatless meatball for our meatless meatball sub at YamChops. We load up a fresh sub bun with meatballs, chipotle-tomato sauce, caramelized onions, caramelized green peppers and a few pickled jalapeño slices.

. . . .

½ cup (45 g) rolled oats

1½ cups (160 g) canned black beans, rinsed and drained

1 tbsp (15 ml) egg replacer mixed with 3 tbsp (45 ml) water

⅓ cup (60 g) fresh or frozen corn kernels, thawed if using frozen

¼ cup (12 g) chopped green onion

¼ cup (45 g) diced red pepper

3 tbsp (40 g) salsa, homemade or store-bought

3 small cloves garlic, minced

2 tsp (5 g) ground cumin

½ tsp dried oregano

½ tsp dried basil

½ tsp smoked paprika

¼ tsp cayenne pepper

⅛ tsp sea salt

Large pinch cinnamon

Large pinch black pepper

Preheat the oven to 350°F (177°C).

Pulse the rolled oats 3 or 4 times in a food processor. Add the rinsed beans and continue to pulse until the beans are roughly chopped. You want to keep some texture in the beans, so be sure not to over-process them.

Whisk the egg replacer and water together until smooth and set it aside to rest for a couple of minutes.

Empty the contents of the processor into a large bowl and add the corn, onion, red pepper, salsa, garlic, cumin, oregano, basil, paprika, cayenne, salt, cinnamon and pepper. Mix together until all ingredients are evenly distributed. Your hands are the best tool for this job.

Add the egg replacer mixture, and mix everything together until the egg replacer mixture is fully incorporated.

Take a small handful of the mixture, a little bigger than a golf ball, and form it into a fairly tight-packed ball. If the mixture holds together, you're good to go. If the mixture is too wet, add 1 to 2 teaspoons (2.5 to 5 g) of pulsed rolled oats. If the mixture is too dry, add 1 to 2 teaspoons (5 to 10 ml) of water. At YamChops, we use a 2 ounce (57 g) scoop to measure these meatballs.

Place the formed meatballs on a parchment paper lined baking sheet and place in your preheated oven for approximately 20 minutes or until firm to the touch. Gently turn the meatballs every 5 minutes to ensure even browning.

Ginger-Miso Meatballs

With a punch of fresh ginger and the earthiness of miso, we love these meatballs as appetizers drizzled with our Soy-Mirin Glaze (page 149).

. . . .

1 tbsp (15 ml) egg replacer mixed with 3 tbsp (45 ml) water

2 tsp (10 ml) tamari or soy sauce

2 tsp (10 g) white miso

1 recipe Seitan Loaf (page 55) or substitute your favorite vegan chick*n strips

¼ cup (12 g) panko

2 tbsp (5 g) minced fresh parsley

1 tbsp (15 g) minced ginger

¼ tsp salt

Preheat the oven to 350°F (177°C).

Whisk the egg replacer with the water and set aside until needed. In a small bowl, mix the tamari and miso together with a fork.

Measure 12 ounces (340 g) of the Seitan Loaf and shred it. Place the shredded seitan in a bowl and mix in the panko, parsley, ginger and salt. Your hands work best from this point forward. Form small handfuls of the mixture into meatballs a little bigger than a golf ball. If the mixture is too wet, add another tablespoon (8 g) of panko; if it's too dry, add 1 to 2 teaspoons (5 to 10 ml) of water.

Lightly spray a parchment paper lined baking sheet with canola oil spray. Place the meatballs on the prepared baking sheet and give them a spray of canola oil spray. Place the baking sheet in the oven for 20 to 25 minutes or until the meatballs are lightly browned. Turn the meatballs halfway through the cooking time.

Drizzle with the Soy-Mirin Glaze (page 149).

The Stack

Magnificence! This is a multi-step, multi-ingredient recipe with a result that absolutely justifies the effort. When news gets out that we're making The Stack—there's no stoppin' the lineups!

. . . .

1 cup (240 ml) Basil Dressing (page 120), or store-bought

2 cups (450 g) Feta Cheeze (page 88), or store-bought

4 cups (600 g) Mozzarella Cheeze (page 144), or store-bought

2 zucchini, ends trimmed

2 yams or sweet potatoes, peeled

2 Yukon Gold potatoes, scrubbed

2 red onions, peeled

Olive oil, for brushing

Sea salt

Freshly ground pepper

1 (10-inch [250-mm]) package soft tortillas

2 roasted red peppers, skinned, seeded and sliced

Lemon Basil Aioli
1 cup (220 g) vegan mayo

Zest and juice of 1 lemon

½ cup (15 g) chopped fresh basil

Tomato Chipotle Sauce
1 (28-oz [806-ml]) can fire roasted diced tomatoes, drained

1 red onion, peeled and chopped

3 large cloves garlic, chopped

1 tbsp (10 g) brown sugar

1 tbsp (13 g) minced chipotle in adobo

¼ cup (7 g) chopped fresh basil

Preheat the oven to 350°F (177°C).

Prepare the Basil Dressing, Feta Cheeze and Mozzarella Cheeze according to the recipe instructions.

To make the lemon basil aioli, whisk the mayo, lemon and basil until everything is completely integrated. Cover the bowl with plastic wrap and store in the refrigerator until needed.

To make the tomato chipotle sauce, place the tomatoes, onion, garlic, brown sugar, chipotle and basil in a large casserole dish and place it in the oven for 45 minutes. Give it a stir every 5 minutes or so. Remove the casserole dish from the oven and spoon the contents into a blender in batches. Carefully blend on high until the sauce is smooth. Place the sauce in a bowl, cover the bowl with plastic wrap and store in the refrigerator until needed.

Preheat the grill to high.

Slice the zucchini, yams and potatoes on a mandoline to a thickness of approximately ⅛ inch (3 mm). Slice the red onion to a thickness of approximately ½ inch (13 mm). Brush all of the veggies with olive oil and sprinkle them with sea salt and freshly ground pepper. Grill in batches until the veggies are tender and nicely marked on both sides. Remove the grilled veggies to a plate.

Let's get stackin'!

Cut a circle of parchment and place it in the bottom of a 10-inch (250-mm) springform pan. Place one tortilla in the bottom of the pan. Spoon on 3 tablespoons (45 ml) of the pesto and spread it over the tortilla. Place a layer of the grilled yams over the pesto. Top the yams with one-fifth of the feta and one-fifth of the mozzarella cheezes.

Place a second tortilla on top and gently push down with your hands. Repeat the pesto—veggie—feta—mozzarella—tortilla layers with the potatoes, onion, red pepper and zucchini. Brush the top tortilla with olive oil and sprinkle with any remaining mozzarella cheeze.

(continued)

The Stack (Cont.)

Tightly cover the springform pan with aluminum foil and place the pan on a baking sheet to catch any drips. Place the pan in the oven and bake for 50 minutes.

Remove from the oven and let it sit covered for 10 minutes. While The Stack is resting, warm the tomato chipotle sauce.

Remove the aluminum foil from the springform pan and run a knife around the inside. Release the latch and remove the form. Slice The Stack into pie-shaped wedges.

Place ¼ cup (60 ml) of the tomato chipotle sauce in the bottom of six shallow bowls or plates. Top with a wedge of The Stack and top the wedge with a heaping tablespoon (15 g) of the aioli.

Not likely, but if there happens to be any leftovers, wrap The Stack in plastic wrap and refrigerate for up to 2 days. Reheat in the oven or microwave.

Pulled BBQ Jackfruit and Carrot

Jackfruit, when cooked, shreds. It's eerily close in texture and appearance to pulled pork. Whip up a batch of BBQ jackfruit, stack it on a burger bun and top it with our Agave-Lime Slaw (page 130) and a squeeze of Chipotle Mayo (page 147). You're sure to satisfy even the staunchest pork lover. Be sure to search out canned young green jackfruit in water or in brine. Jackfruit packed in syrup is a no-go for this recipe.

2 tbsp (30 ml) olive oil, plus more for greasing

1 (20-oz [280-g]) can young green jackfruit in water or brine

1 medium sweet onion, thinly sliced

4 small cloves garlic, thinly sliced

1 cup (50 g) grated carrot

¾ cup (177 ml) vegetable stock

1 cup (240 ml) BBQ sauce, divided

Preheat the oven to 350°F (177°C). Lightly oil a parchment paper lined baking sheet.

Drain and rinse the jackfruit. Cutting from the core to the point, slice the jackfruit wedges into smaller wedges, about ½ inch (13 mm) at the wide end.

Set a large skillet over medium-high heat and add the olive oil. When the oil is hot, add the onion and garlic. Sauté for 7 minutes or until the onions are just beginning to brown. Add the jackfruit and the carrots to the skillet and continue to sauté, stirring regularly, for 4 minutes. Add the stock and continue to cook for 12 minutes or until the jackfruit is soft enough to be mashed with a potato masher. Most, or all, of the stock will have cooked off.

Remove the jackfruit mixture from the heat and empty it onto the prepared baking sheet. Mash with a potato masher until the jackfruit shreds into a pulled pork texture.

Spread the jackfruit mixture out on the baking sheet and place it in the oven for 12 minutes, mixing everything around a few times along the way. The edges of some of the jackfruit mixture will start to crisp and darken—that's what you're going for. Remove the baking sheet from the oven and pour half of the BBQ sauce over the jackfruit mixture. Mix everything together with a spatula and return the baking sheet to the oven for an additional 12 minutes.

Remove the baking sheet and mix in the remaining half of the BBQ sauce.

Now . . . where are those buns?

Tofu Makhani

This is our vegan version of the classic East Indian dish Butter Chicken. Rich and deeply flavored, this tomato- and cashew cream–based makhani will keep 'em coming back for more!

. . . .

2 (416-g) blocks extra firm tofu (see note)

½ cup (115 g) vegan butter

2 cups (300 g) diced sweet onion

4 large cloves garlic, minced

¼ cup + 1 tbsp (45 g) garam masala

2 tbsp (15 g) ground ginger

2 tbsp (15 g) Mexican chili powder

2 tsp (6 g) ground turmeric

1 tsp cayenne pepper

1 (28-oz [806-ml]) can diced tomatoes

1 cup (240 ml) Cashew Sour Cream (page 140)

¾ cup (170 g) tomato paste

1 tbsp (15 g) sea salt

1 to 1½ cups (240 to 360 ml) water

Cut the tofu in ½-inch (13-mm) cubes and set aside until needed.

Melt the butter in a large pot over medium heat. Add the onions and garlic, and sauté for 5 minutes, or until the onions are lightly colored. Add the garam masala, ginger, chili powder, turmeric and cayenne, and sauté for 2 minutes, stirring constantly. Add the tomatoes and continue to sauté for 5 minutes or until the tomatoes begin to break down.

Add the Cashew Sour Cream, tomato paste and salt to the pot and mix well. Reduce the heat to low and cook for 5 minutes, stirring regularly. Add the tofu cubes and 1 cup (240 ml) of the water. Cook for 30 minutes, mixing gently and often. Add additional water as necessary to reach your preferred consistency.

We like it thick and served hot over jasmine rice.

Note: Always search out non-GMO tofu for tofu recipes.

Chick*n-Fried Baked Portobello

Serve these cutlets with a side of mashed potatoes, sautéed greens and a whole lotta Mushroom-Shallot Gravy (page 148).

. . . .

3 tbsp (45 ml) egg replacer whisked with 9 tbsp (133 ml) warm water

4 large or 8 medium portobello mushrooms

1 cup (128 g) unbleached all-purpose flour

1 tsp coarse grind pepper (sometimes called butcher's grind)

1 tsp Spanish paprika

¼ tsp garlic powder

¼ tsp onion powder

Preheat the oven to 350°F (177°C).

Whisk together the egg replacer and the water in a flat bowl and set aside until needed.

While the oven is preheating, do a bit of cosmetic work on the portobellos. First, remove the stems. Then, starting at the inside edge of the portobello cap, grab the skin and slowly pull it back to peel the mushroom. Next, flip the cap over and with a small spoon, gently scrape away the gills. Finally, slice off any of the cap's overhang so that the cap sits flat.

Mix the flour, pepper, paprika, garlic powder and onion powder together in a second flat bowl. Lightly spray a parchment paper lined baking sheet with canola oil.

Dip a portobello cap into the egg replacer mixture and move it all about until the entire surface of both sides of the cap is coated. Place the cap into the flour mixture to coat it. Shake off any excess flour and place the cap on the prepared baking sheet. Continue the process with the remaining caps.

Spray the portobellos with canola spray and place the baking sheet in the oven. Bake for 12 to 15 minutes or until the mushrooms are soft and the breading is crisp and lightly colored.

Plant-Based Chick*n

Our most versatile plant-based meat. We use this *&^% in everything.

. . . .

1¼ cups (300 ml) water

2 tsp (4 g) vegan chicken bouillon powder

1 tbsp (15 ml) olive oil

1 tbsp (15 ml) vegan Worcestershire sauce

1½ cups (216 g) vital wheat gluten

3 tbsp (18 g) almond flour (see note), plus more for dusting

3 tbsp (9 g) nutritional yeast

1½ tsp (15 g) poultry seasoning

1½ tsp (12 g) garlic powder

½ tsp smoked paprika

½ tsp onion powder

½ tsp sea salt

Whisk the water, bouillon, olive oil and Worcestershire sauce together in a medium bowl.

Combine the vital wheat gluten, almond flour, nutritional yeast, poultry seasoning, garlic powder, paprika, onion powder and salt in a large bowl. Add the wet ingredients and knead the mixture in the bowl until the wet and dry ingredients are fully incorporated.

Lightly dust the countertop with almond flour and knead the dough for 10 minutes. Alternatively, you can place the dough in the bowl of a stand mixer fitted with a dough hook. The dough should be a bit damp, but should not stick to your fingers. If it is sticking to your fingers, add 1 to 2 teaspoons (2.5 to 5 g) of almond flour. Shape the dough into a loaf, cover it with a clean towel and let it rest on your counter for 30 minutes.

In a pot large enough to hold the loaf, add 2 inches (50 mm) of water and bring the water to a boil. Set a steamer basket inside the pot. Loosely wrap the loaf in aluminum foil and place the wrapped loaf in the steamer basket. Cover the pot and let it steam for 20 minutes. Gently flip the loaf after 10 minutes.

Check your water level from time to time to make sure you don't steam the pot dry. Add additional water if necessary.

Remove the loaf from the pot and let it cool to room temperature.

Note: You can make your own almond flour. Place 1 cup (170 g) of raw almonds in a food processor or blender. Pulse in 15-second spurts to grind the almonds into a powder. Be careful not to go beyond the powder stage or you'll end up with almond butter. All things considered, that's not such a bad thing—but for this recipe you're just going for a flour.

THERE'S AN APP FOR THAT

Selfie-Worthy Appetizers and Sides

Yes, these apps make wonderful starters and passed hors d'oeuvres—
and yes, these sides make any meal that much better—but, if the truth be
known, we often forego the main and make a meal of nothing
but these little selfie-worthy dishes.

Ba-con—4 Ways

Growing up, I was never a fan of bacon, but it was clear to me early on that I was definitely in the minority! If you were (or are) part of the majority, here are four ways to keep bacon alive in your life—and pigs alive for theirs.

- -

Tempeh Ba-con

1 (8-oz [227-g]) package organic tempeh

¼ cup (60 ml) tamari or soy sauce

¼ cup (60 ml) maple syrup

2½ tsp (13 ml) hickory liquid smoke

2 tsp (5 g) onion powder

1 tsp fresh garlic, minced

1 tsp Spanish paprika

½ tsp coarse grind pepper (sometimes called butcher's grind)

2 tbsp (30 ml) canola oil, divided

Coconut Ba-con

2 tbsp (30 ml) tamari or soy sauce

2 tbsp (30 ml) maple syrup

1 tbsp (15 ml) hickory liquid smoke

1 tbsp (15 ml) vegan Worcestershire sauce

1 tsp smoked sea salt

1 tsp coarse grind pepper (sometimes called butcher's grind)

4 cups (300 g) organic unsweetened coconut flakes (see note)

Tempeh Ba-con

Steam the tempeh in a steamer basket for 15 minutes. Carefully remove the tempeh to your cutting board and allow it to cool for 15 minutes.

While the tempeh is cooling, prepare the marinade. Whisk together the tamari, maple syrup, liquid smoke, onion powder, garlic, paprika and pepper. When the tempeh has cooled, slice it into ¼-inch (6-mm)-thick strips with a very sharp knife. Pour half of the marinade into a shallow baking dish and gently lay the tempeh strips in a single layer. Pour the remaining marinade over top of the tempeh. Let the tempeh marinate for a minimum of 4 hours, preferably overnight.

Heat 1 tablespoon (15 ml) of the oil over medium heat in a non-stick pan. When the oil is hot, remove the tempeh from the marinade and let it drain for a minute on paper towel. Gently place the tempeh strips in the hot oil and cook for 3 to 4 minutes until they are golden brown and crispy (do not crowd the pan). Carefully flip the tempeh strips and cook for 2 to 3 minutes until the second side is golden brown and crispy. Repeat with the remaining tempeh strips, adding additional oil as needed. Drain the strips on paper towel.

Coconut Ba-con

Preheat the oven to 325°F (163°C).

Mix the tamari, maple syrup, liquid smoke, Worcestershire sauce, salt and pepper until fully combined. Add the coconut flakes and mix well to coat all flakes with the marinade. Your hands work best for this.

Spread the coconut flakes in a single layer about ¾-inch (19-mm) thick on a parchment lined sheet pan. Bake for approximately 20 minutes until the flakes are a deep golden brown. Mix every 5 minutes and more often as you're nearing the end of the cooking cycle.

Note: Hunt down coconut flakes (sometimes called coconut chips) for this recipe. Shredded coconut does not work.

(continued)

Ba-con—4 Ways (Cont.)

Shiitake Mushroom Ba-con

1 lb (454 g) shiitake mushrooms, stems removed

½ cup (120 ml) tamari or soy sauce

2 tbsp (30 ml) olive oil

2 tbsp (30 ml) maple syrup

1 tbsp (15 ml) hickory liquid smoke

1 tsp smoked paprika

1 tsp onion powder

½ tsp garlic powder

½ tsp smoked sea salt

Rice Paper Ba-con

¼ cup (60 ml) tamari or soy sauce

2 tbsp (30 ml) olive oil

2 tbsp (30 ml) maple syrup

1 tbsp (15 ml) hot water

1 tbsp (15 ml) hickory liquid smoke

1 tbsp (3 g) nutritional yeast

1 tsp smoked paprika

½ tsp garlic powder

12 pieces rice paper

Shiitake Mushroom Ba-con

Preheat the oven to 400°F (204°C).

Slice the shiitake mushroom caps into ¼-inch (6-mm) slices and place them in a large bowl.

Whisk together the tamari, olive oil, maple syrup, liquid smoke, paprika, onion powder, garlic powder and salt in a medium bowl. Add the marinade to the shiitake mushrooms and mix well to make sure all mushrooms are coated. Let the mushrooms rest for 15 minutes to soak up the marinade.

Spread the mushrooms out in a single layer on a parchment lined sheet pan. (Do not crowd.) Bake for 14 minutes, flip the mushrooms and return the pan to the oven for an additional 14 minutes or until the edges are beginning to blacken and crisp up. Remove the mushrooms to a paper towel lined plate and leave to cool. The mushrooms will crisp up as they cool.

Rice Paper Ba-con

Preheat the oven to 400°F (204°C).

Whisk the tamari, oil, maple syrup, water, liquid smoke, nutritional yeast, paprika and garlic powder together in a flat bowl that is large enough to allow you to submerge a sheet of rice paper. Place 2 sheets of rice paper in the marinade and allow them to soften for 30 seconds. Remove the rice paper sheets, lay them on top of each other on a cutting board and press them together gently. With a very sharp knife cut the rice paper into 1- to 1½-inch (25- to 37-mm) strips. Repeat with the remaining rice paper.

Place the strips on a parchment lined baking sheet and bake for 6 to 7 minutes until crisp. Keep a close eye on the strips as they can go from delightful to destroyed in an instant.

Tomato Sashimi

I was asked to be the spokesperson for Near You, a local summer produce campaign in Ontario. This is one of the recipes I developed featuring heirloom tomatoes.

. . . .

2 medium heirloom tomatoes, ripe but firm

½ cup (120 ml) rice vinegar

¼ cup (62 g) evaporated cane sugar

1 cup (220 g) sushi rice

3 tbsp (45 ml) marinade (rice vinegar and cane sugar from tomato fillets)

2 tsp (5 g) powdered sugar

1 tsp wasabi powder

1 tsp water

1 sheet sushi nori, cut into ½-inch (13-mm) strips

Pickled ginger, for garnish

Bring a large pot of water to a boil over high heat. Prepare an ice bath by filling a large bowl with a couple of cups of ice cubes and cold water.

With a serrated knife, cut a ½-inch (13-mm) X in the base of each tomato (opposite the stem end). You just want to break the skin with your knife. Carefully place the tomatoes in the boiling water with a slotted spoon for 30 to 40 seconds or until the skin just begins to separate where you cut the X. Immediately remove the tomatoes from the boiling water and plunge them into the ice bath to halt the cooking.

Once the tomatoes have cooled completely, remove them from the ice bath and gently peel away the skin starting at the X. Slice the peeled tomatoes into 6 or 8 wedges (depending on the size of your tomatoes). You're after a wedge about the size of tuna or salmon fillets used in traditional sashimi. Remove the seeds and inner membrane from the wedges so that you are left with a flat tomato fillet.

Heat the rice vinegar and cane sugar in a small pot over medium heat. Stir constantly for 6 to 7 minutes until the sugar melts. Transfer the marinade to a medium bowl. Add the tomato fillets to the bowl, cover with plastic wrap and allow the tomato fillets to marinate at room temperature for 1 hour.

Bring 1½ cups (360 ml) of water to a boil and add the sushi rice. Stir once, reduce the heat to low, cover the pot and cook the rice for 20 minutes or until the rice has absorbed all of the water and is tender (not mushy) to the bite.

Place the rice in a glass bowl and add 3 tablespoons (45 ml) of the tomato fillet marinade. With a wooden spoon, gently fold the marinade into the rice. Let the rice cool slightly.

Mix the powdered sugar, wasabi and water together in a small bowl and set aside for 15 minutes for the flavors to meld.

Time to make some sashimi! With damp hands, place a generous spoonful of rice in the palm of one hand. Very gently squeeze the rice into a football shape. Actually, it should be a bit more of a rugby ball shape, and it should be sized so you can pop the whole thing in your mouth in one fell swoop.

Lay a tomato fillet across each rice rugby ball. Dampen one end of one of the nori strips and wrap the strip around the circumference of the sashimi, trimming off any overlap with scissors. Repeat with the remaining sashimi.

Top with a dab of sugared wasabi and serve with pickled ginger on the side.

Carrot Lox

Acknowledged by wild salmon across North America with a Two Fins Up rating, our Carrot Lox is made with organic carrots and our own secret (until now) marinade. Layer it on a bagel and top it off with capers, red onion, fresh dill and Cashew Sour Cream (page 140).

. . . .

3 lb (1.3 kg) large carrots

2 tbsp (30 g) smoked sea salt

2 tbsp (18 g) brown sugar

1 ½ tsp (4 g) cracked black pepper

3 tbsp (45 ml) egg replacer mixed with 9 tbsp (133 ml) warm water

Zest of 2 lemons

3 tbsp (45 ml) olive oil

Peel the carrots and thinly slice them lengthwise to approximately ⅛-inch (3-mm) thick. A mandoline works best for this step.

Mix together the salt, sugar and pepper in a small bowl. Place a single layer of the carrots in a large bowl and generously dust with the seasoning mix. Place a second layer of the carrots over the first and generously dust with the seasoning mix. Repeat until all of the carrots are dusted with the seasoning mix. Let the carrots marinate for 1 hour.

Preheat the oven to 350°F (177°C).

Whisk together the egg replacer, water, lemon zest and oil in a bowl. Let the mixture rest for 10 minutes.

With your hands, remove the carrot slices from the bowl and transfer them to a clean bowl. Empty the water that has accumulated in the base of the bowl through a sieve. Add the spices collected in the sieve back into the bowl of carrots.

Whisk the resting egg replacer mixture a couple of times and add it to the bowl of carrots. Gently mix the carrots and egg replacer mixture together so that all of the carrot slices are coated.

Lay one carrot slice on a parchment paper lined–baking sheet. Lay a second carrot slice overlapping the previous slice by three-quarters. Lay a third slice overlapping the second slice by three-quarters, and a fourth, and a fifth, and a sixth . . . until all of the carrots are laid out.

Tightly cover the baking sheet with aluminum foil and place it in the oven for 45 minutes. Remove the baking sheet from the oven and let the carrots cool completely. Do not remove the tinfoil until the carrots have cooled, about 30 minutes. (No peeking either.)

Once cooled, remove the aluminum foil and make a beeline for a fresh bagel!

Fiesta Potatoes

Another recipe developed for the Near You local produce campaign—this one featuring a new crop, mini red potatoes. I often make a whole meal of these one-bite flavor fiestas, but where they really shine is as an appetizer followed by our Fishless Tacos (page 45).

16–24 mini red potatoes

2 tbsp (30 ml) olive oil

1 tsp sea salt

⅓ cup (78 ml) salsa (at YamChops, we use chipotle salsa)

¼ cup (60 ml) Cashew Sour Cream (page 140)

2 tbsp (6 g) chopped green onion

Taco Meat

½ cup (65 g) walnuts

¾ tsp Mexican chili powder

¼ tsp ground cumin

⅛ tsp sea salt

Large pinch of cayenne pepper

1 tbsp (15 ml) olive oil

Preheat the oven to 350°F (177°C).

Bring a large pot of water to a boil and carefully add the potatoes using a slotted spoon. Boil for approximately 12 minutes or until the potatoes can be easily pierced with a skewer. The cooking time will vary depending on the size of the potatoes. Drain the potatoes and run them under cold water for a couple of minutes to halt the cooking process.

To make the taco meat, place the walnuts on a parchment paper lined baking sheet and place in the oven for 5 to 7 minutes or until they have darkened slightly and they smell toasty. Remove the walnuts from the oven and place them in a mini food processor along with the chili powder, cumin, salt and cayenne pepper. Pulse the walnuts 2 or 3 times. Add the olive oil and pulse 2 or 3 more times. You're after a coarsely ground nut about the size of a peppercorn.

Set the oven to broil.

Place a cooked mini potato on a clean cutting board. Grab a clean cotton towel and fold it into a square. Place the towel over the potato, and with the palm of your hand, push down in one quick movement to smash the potato. You want the potatoes to be ¼- to ⅓-inch (6- to 8-mm) thick. Lightly brush the smashed potatoes on both sides with the olive oil and place them on a parchment paper lined baking sheet. Sprinkle the potatoes with the salt and place the baking sheet under the broiler for 3 to 4 minutes or until the edges of the potatoes just begin to get crispy.

And now, for the perfect mouthful—working quickly, top each smashed potato with 2 teaspoons (5 g) of the walnut taco meat, 1 teaspoon of salsa, 1 teaspoon of Cashew Sour Cream and a sprinkle of green onions.

Hunan Dumplings

We serve these little bundles of flavor pot sticker style—but feel free to steam them or deep-fry them, if you prefer. Whip up a quick Soy-Mirin Glaze (page 149) or Peanut Sauce (page 143) to serve alongside these dumplings.

Serves 6 as an appetizer

½ recipe (185 g) Plant-Based Chick*n (page 69) or substitute your favorite vegan chick*n

⅓ cup (78 ml) maple syrup

¼ cup (12 g) chopped green onions

3 tbsp (43 g) sambal oelek

3 small cloves garlic, chopped

2 tbsp (30 ml) sesame oil

2 tbsp (30 g) peeled chopped ginger

½ tsp sea salt

1 tbsp (10 g) cornstarch

1 (7.5-oz [220-g]) package round dumpling wrappers

1 tbsp (15 ml) grape-seed or canola oil

3 to 4 tbsp (45 to 60 ml) water, plus more for wrappers

Sliced green onions and sesame seeds, for garnish

Cut the chick*n into pieces and place it in your food processor. Pulse the chick*n 4 or 5 times to roughly chop it. Add the maple syrup, onions, sambal oelek, garlic, sesame oil, ginger and salt to the processor and pulse until the mixture just comes together. You want to keep some texture in the mixture.

Fill a small bowl with warm water. Line a baking sheet with parchment paper and lightly sprinkle cornstarch over the parchment.

Lay 4 dumpling wrappers on the counter. Keep the remaining dumpling wrappers covered with a damp towel to keep them from drying out. Place a heaping tablespoon (15 g) of the chick*n filling in the center of each wrapper. With a brush or your fingertips, dampen the outer ½ inch (13 mm) of the dumpling wrapper with the water. Fold the edge closest to you over the filling to meet the opposite side. Gently squeeze out any air bubbles with your fingertips and seal the edges using a fork. (Or if you have one of those plastic dumpling presses, now's the time to dig it out.) Place the dumplings on the prepared baking sheet standing them on their flat ends. Repeat with the remaining filling and dumpling wrappers.

Place a large skillet over medium heat and add the grape-seed oil. Place the dumplings, standing on their flat ends, in the skillet and cook them for 4 to 5 minutes or until the bottom is crisp and golden. Add the water and cover the skillet to steam the dumplings for 3 minutes or until all of the water has cooked off.

Serve on a platter sprinkled with green onions and sesame seeds.

Thai Leaf Snacks

I had this dish for the first time at an amazing vegan Thai-fusion restaurant in Montreal called ChuChai. This is my version of their Thai snack *miang kham*. Classically, the ingredients are wrapped in a betel leaf (cha-ploo) with the sauce spooned over the top. You can substitute red spinach leaves for the betel leaf, or you can house it all in a little filo cup like I do. This little beauty defines the term layers of flavors! And, as a bonus, you get to practice your knife skills too!

¼ cup (60 ml) melted vegan butter or canola oil spray

1 (16-oz [454-g]) package filo dough, thawed overnight in the refrigerator

¼ cup (25 g) finely diced shallot, divided

¼ cup (60 g) finely diced ginger, divided

¼ cup (20 g) shredded coconut

¼ cup (40 g) peanuts or cashews

¼ cup (55 g) brown sugar

2 tbsp (30 ml) mushroom soy sauce

1 tbsp (15 ml) hot water

¼ tsp white pepper

24 baby spinach leaves

Preheat the oven to 300°F (149°C). Lightly brush a mini muffin tray with the melted vegan butter.

Working quickly, carefully unwrap the filo and gently lay one sheet flat on a cutting board. Brush with the butter. Gently lay a second sheet of filo on top of the first and lightly brush with the butter. Repeat a third time. Reroll the remaining filo and wrap in a slightly damp, clean kitchen towel to keep it from drying out.

With a sharp knife, cut the stacked filo sheets into approximately 3-inch (75-mm) squares. Place a square over a muffin cup and gently push the filo into the form. Repeat to fill all muffin cups. Place the muffin tray in the oven and bake until golden, approximately 9 to 11 minutes. Remove the filo cups from the oven and set aside.

Set aside the shallot and ginger in two small bowls. Lightly toast the coconut in a dry pan for 4 to 5 minutes over medium-low heat until it is just golden in color. Remove from the heat and set aside in a small bowl. Lightly toast the peanuts for 6 to 8 minutes until golden. Remove the peanuts from the heat and pulse a few times in a food processor. Set aside in a small bowl.

To make the sauce, add the brown sugar, soy sauce, 1 tablespoon (15 g) each of shallot and ginger, water and white pepper to a small sauce pot over medium-low heat. Heat, stirring regularly for approximately 8 minutes, until the brown sugar has melted and the sauce has thickened slightly. Remove the sauce from the heat and set aside in a small bowl.

For the perfect bite, place 1 spinach leaf in the bottom of each of the filo cups. Spoon in ½ teaspoon of the shallot, ½ teaspoon of the ginger, ½ teaspoon of the coconut, 1 teaspoon of the peanut and top it off with 1 teaspoon of the sauce.

Note: The filo cups can be assembled up to 3 hours in advance. Top with the sauce right before serving.

Lemon Pepper, Double Mustard, Roasted Yukon Wedges

I'm convinced that I've created almost all of my sauce and dressing recipes based on their compatibility with roasted Yukon Gold wedges. Is it wrong to love a yellow-fleshed spud so much? This particular sauce is spectacular on roasted wedges and it's also great on grilled veggies, especially asparagus, and grains, especially quinoa. Or just stick to the roasted wedges . . . you won't be sorry!

• •

6 large Yukon Gold or other yellow-fleshed potato

3 tbsp (45 ml) olive oil

2 tbsp (5 g) fresh rosemary, finely chopped

1 tsp sea salt

½ tsp freshly ground pepper

2 tbsp (5 g) flat leaf parsley, finely chopped, for garnish

Dressing

¼ cup (60 ml) smooth Dijon mustard (see note)

¼ cup (60 ml) grainy Dijon mustard

3 tbsp (45 ml) agave syrup

4 tsp (13 g) garlic, minced

2 tsp (4 g) lemon pepper

½ tsp Greek seasoning

¼ tsp sea salt

¼ tsp freshly ground pepper

1¼ cups (295 ml) canola oil

¼ cup (60 ml) fresh lemon juice

2 tbsp (19 g) lemon zest

Preheat the oven to 400°F (204°C).

Wash the potatoes and dry them well. With a sharp knife, carefully slice each potato into 8 wedges. Place the wedges in a large bowl and add the olive oil. Toss the wedges to coat them well with the oil. Sprinkle with the rosemary, salt and pepper and toss again. Set aside.

To prepare the dressing, add the mustards, agave, garlic, lemon pepper, Greek seasoning, salt and pepper in a food processor. Pulse a few times to blend the ingredients. With the processor running, add the oil slowly in a steady stream. Process until the dressing is emulsified. Add the lemon juice and lemon zest and pulse 3 or 4 times to incorporate. The dressing should be thick, but still pourable. Empty the dressing into a bowl, cover with plastic wrap and refrigerate until needed.

Line two sheet pans with parchment paper and stand the wedges up with the skin side down. Place them in your oven and roast until the wedges are tender and golden brown, about 35 to 40 minutes. Remove and brush each wedge generously with the dressing. Return to the oven for 10 additional minutes.

Remove the wedges to your serving platter and drizzle generously with the dressing. Serve additional dressing on the side. Garnish with the chopped parsley.

Note: You can use all smooth Dijon for this recipe by substituting 2 additional tablespoons (30 ml) of smooth Dijon in place of the grainy Dijon.

Gingery Tofu Fries

It's a constant battle to protect these gingery-sweet fries from sticky-fingered staff that just happen to walk by when a fresh batch comes out of the oven. They make a wonderful side for any Asian-inspired meal and work equally well as a main with a crunchy slaw. Lately, we've been combining them with our purple cabbage slaw and mango salsa (see our Fishless Tacos recipe, page 45) and serving them up as a taco.

· ·

1 (416-g) block extra firm tofu (see note)

Grape-seed or canola oil, for shallow frying

Cornstarch, to coat

1 cup (240 ml) organic ketchup

¼ cup (62 g) evaporated cane sugar

¼ cup (60 ml) tamari or soy sauce

3 tbsp (45 g) finely chopped ginger

2 tsp (10 g) sambal oelek

½ tsp coarse grind pepper (sometimes called butcher's grind)

Preheat the oven to 325°F (163°C).

Drain and press the tofu for 15 minutes (see note). Cut the tofu into "fries," measuring roughly ½ x ½ x 3 inches (13 x 13 x 76 mm).

Heat about ¼ inch (6 mm) of oil in a frying pan over medium heat. Place 2 or 3 tablespoons (19 to 28 g) of cornstarch in a plastic zip bag, add a few tofu fries and shake 'em up. When the oil is hot, remove the fries from the bag using tongs, shake off any excess cornstarch and carefully place them into the oil. Do not crowd the pan. Cook, turning the tofu until the fries are golden on all sides, approximately 1 to 1½ minutes per side. Let the tofu fries drain on paper towels.

Prepare the sauce by combining the ketchup, sugar, tamari, ginger, sambal and pepper in a saucepot over medium heat. Stir well. Bring the sauce to a light boil, stirring regularly, then turn the heat down to simmer. Cook, stirring occasionally, for approximately 10 minutes or until the sauce has thickened slightly.

Place the drained tofu fries on a baking dish in a single layer. Spoon the sauce over top of the fries, turning them so that all sides are coated. Place the baking dish in the oven and bake for 25 to 30 minutes or until the tofu has puffed slightly and the sauce has formed a thick and sticky coating.

Note: Always search out non-GMO tofu for tofu recipes. To press the tofu, wrap the blocks in a double layer of paper towels. Place the wrapped tofu on a cutting board with a plate or sheet pan on top. Weigh down the tofu by placing 2 or 3 cans (cans of tomatoes or beans work great) on top of the plate or sheet pan and let rest for 15 minutes.

Nacho Cheeze

Imagine the perfect bowl: nacho chips, black beans, diced tomatoes, grated carrots, roasted corn kernels, pickled avocado, pickled onions, pickled jalapeño, a hefty ladle of Nacho Cheeze and a swirl of Cashew Sour Cream (page 140). Turn the game on and enjoy!

Approximately 2 cups (480 ml)

2 large peeled russet potatoes

¾ cup (130 g) peeled carrot

¾ cup (32 g) nutritional yeast

⅓ cup (80 ml) olive oil

⅓ cup (80 ml) water

3 tbsp (45 ml) lemon juice

½ tsp onion powder

¼ tsp garlic powder

¼ tsp turmeric powder

Bring a large pot of salted water to a boil. Cut the potatoes and carrots into 1-inch (25-mm) chunks.

When the water is boiling, add the potatoes and carrots and boil uncovered for 20 minutes or until the potatoes are easily pierced with a skewer. Drain in a colander.

Place the drained potatoes and carrots into a high-speed blender along with the nutritional yeast, olive oil, water, lemon juice, onion powder, garlic powder and turmeric powder. Blend, scraping down the sides of the blender a couple of times, until the cheeze is smooth and creamy.

The cheeze should be a thick, pourable consistency. If the cheeze is too thick, you can thin the cheeze by blending in 1 or 2 tablespoons (15 to 30 ml) of water.

Note: If refrigerated, the cheeze should be reheated over very low heat for 5 to 7 minutes until you reach your desired temperature and consistency.

Perfect Brown Rice

Serves 6

We found that cooking our brown rice like pasta is the way to get it right—every time! The rice moving about in the bubbling water seems to give it the room it needs to achieve maximum puffiness and minimum mushiness.

12 cups (2.8 L) water

2 cups (370 g) long grain brown rice

1 tsp sea salt

Bring the water to a boil in a large pot.

Rinse the rice in a strainer for 30 seconds under cold running water. When the water is boiling, add the salt and the rice and stir once. Let the rice boil, uncovered, for 55 minutes.

Drain the rice in a strainer for 10 seconds and return it to the same pot that it was cooked in (off the heat). Cover the pot and allow the rice to rest and steam away any remaining water for 20 minutes.

Fluff the rice with a fork and transfer to your serving bowl.

Tunaless Tuna Salad

To this day, I have fond childhood memories of my grandmother's double-deckers: white bread topped with tuna salad, topped with white bread, topped with egg salad, topped with white bread. Needless to say, she cut the crust off for us grandkids too!

. . . .

1 (19-oz [540-ml]) can chickpeas, rinsed

2 tbsp (25 g) finely diced red onion

2 tbsp (25 g) finely diced celery

1 tbsp (10 g) finely diced dill pickle

2 tsp (2 g) finely chopped fresh dill

2 tsp (2 g) finely chopped fresh parsley

2 tsp (4 g) surfine capers, rinsed (see notes)

2 tsp (1 g) nori flakes (see notes)

½ tsp sea salt

¼ tsp coarse grind pepper (sometimes called butcher's grind)

¼ cup + 2 tbsp (87 ml) vegan mayo

Eggless Egg Salad (page 91), for serving

Bread, for serving

Sprouts, for serving

Red onion slices, for serving

Sliced tomatoes, for serving

Place the chickpeas in a large bowl and mash them with a potato masher until you reach a tuna-like consistency.

Add the red onion, celery, pickle, dill, parsley, capers, nori flakes, salt and pepper and mix well to evenly distribute the ingredients. Add the mayo and mix well to incorporate.

Take some tuna salad, egg salad and white bread, and build your own double decker. Make it a complete sandwich by adding sprouts, red onion and tomato slices.

Notes: Surfine capers are pickled young to retain their flavor and texture. They are about the size of a small pea. If you can only find the larger capote, capucine, fine or grusas capers, that's OK—just be sure to cut them into pea-size pieces.

If you don't have nori flakes, you can pulse a 2-inch (50-mm) square of sushi nori in your spice grinder or break it into very small pieces with your fingers.

Feta Cheeze

What's a Greek salad, cheeze platter or The Stack (page 60) without feta? Fear not … this feta keeps the Greek in your salad, the tang on your cheeze platter and the creaminess in The Stack.

Makes about 3 cups (370 g) crumbled

1 (416-g) block extra firm tofu (see note)

½ cup (118 ml) melted coconut oil

3 tbsp (45 ml) fresh lemon juice

2 tbsp (30 ml) apple cider vinegar

2½ tsp (13 g) sea salt

2 tsp (1 g) dried basil

2 tsp (1 g) dried oregano

½ tsp onion powder

Drain and press the tofu for 30 minutes. You want the tofu to be as dry as possible.

Select some molds that you will use to shape the cheeze. At YamChops, we use 12-ounce (340-g) plastic deli containers lined with plastic wrap as molds. Onion soup bowls lined with plastic wrap also work great. Leave some plastic wrap overhanging the rim of your molds. This will help in removing the cheeze once it has set.

Crumble the tofu with your hands into a food processor. Add the melted coconut oil and process until the mixture is smooth. Add the lemon juice, vinegar, salt, basil, oregano and onion powder, and pulse 5 or 6 times to mix everything together.

Spoon the mixture into the prepared molds, packing it down tightly with the back of a spoon. Cover with plastic wrap and refrigerate for a minimum of 6 hours to allow the cheeze to set.

Note: Always search out non-GMO tofu for tofu recipes. To press the tofu, wrap the blocks in a double layer of paper towels. Place the wrapped tofu on a cutting board with a plate or sheet pan on top. Weigh down the tofu by placing 2 or 3 cans (cans of tomatoes or beans work great) on top of the plate or sheet pan and let rest for 30 minutes.

Szechuan Green Beans

Quick . . . crunchy . . . and totally nibble-able. This recipe delivers a medium heat level, but feel free to adjust the heat up or down to please your inner Scoville scale.

. . . .

1 lb (454 g) green beans, ends trimmed

1 tbsp (15 ml) grape-seed or canola oil

½ cup (75 g) coarsely chopped sweet onion

1 tbsp (10 g) toasted sesame seeds, for garnish

Sauce

1 tbsp (15 ml) sesame oil

¼ cup (60 ml) vegan hoisin sauce

2 tbsp (30 ml) soy sauce

1 tbsp (15 ml) water

2 tsp (10 g) minced ginger

2 small cloves garlic, minced

2 tsp (8 g) evaporated cane sugar

2 tsp (10 g) chili paste with garlic or ¼ tsp red chili flakes

Bring a large pot of water to a boil. Prepare an ice bath by filling a large bowl with cold water and adding 2 to 3 large handfuls of ice.

Once the water is boiling, add the green beans and cook for 3 minutes. Immediately remove the green beans and plunge them into the ice bath to halt the cooking process. When cool, remove the green beans from the ice bath and spread them out on a clean towel to drain.

Prepare the sauce by whisking together the sesame oil, hoisin, soy sauce, water, ginger, garlic, sugar and chili paste in bowl. You're looking for a pancake batter consistency. If the sauce is too thick, you can whisk in another tablespoon (15 ml) of water.

Heat the grape-seed oil in a wok or large skillet over medium-high heat. When the oil is hot, add the green beans and the onions to the wok. Stir fry for 7 to 9 minutes, or until the green beans have started to blacken in spots.

Turn the heat down to low and add the sauce. Mix everything together to evenly coat the beans in the sauce and cook for 2 to 3 minutes or until the sauce thickly clings to the beans.

Transfer the green beans to a serving plate and top with toasted sesame seeds.

Eggless Egg Salad

Be sure to search out kala namak for this recipe. It is a South Asian, pungent-smelling rock salt, and it delivers an authentic egg salad umami. It's often referred to as Indian black salt but, when searching it out, keep in mind that it's actually pink! Pair this recipe with our Tunaless Tuna Salad (page 86) and build yourself one of my childhood faves: a double-decker sandwich.

• •

1 (416-g) block extra firm tofu (see note)

½ cup (115 g) finely diced celery

⅓ cup (50 g) finely diced dill pickle

1 tsp kala namak

¼ cup + 2 tbsp (87 ml) vegan mayo

1 tbsp (15 ml) apple cider vinegar

2 tsp (11 g) Dijon mustard

2 tsp (5 g) celery seed

2 tsp (8 g) evaporated cane sugar

2 tsp (5 g) onion powder

1 tsp garlic powder

1 tsp ground turmeric

½ tsp coarse grind pepper (sometimes called butcher's grind)

Drain and press the tofu. Break the pressed tofu in pieces into a large bowl. Mash the tofu with a potato masher until you reach an egg salad-like consistency. Add the celery and pickle. Sprinkle the kala namak over the tofu and mix well with a spatula to fully distribute the ingredients.

In a separate bowl, whisk together the mayo, vinegar, mustard, celery seed, sugar, onion powder, garlic powder, turmeric and pepper. Add the dressing to the tofu mixture and mix together well.

Note: Always search out non-GMO tofu for tofu recipes. To press the tofu, wrap the blocks in a double layer of paper towels. Place the wrapped tofu on a cutting board with a plate or sheet pan on top. Weigh down the tofu by placing 2 or 3 cans (cans of tomatoes or beans work great) on top of the plate or sheet pan and let rest for 15 minutes.

Creamless Creamed Corn

You can use frozen corn for this dish, but fresh summer corn kernels cut off the cob makes it extra special! It's a wonderful side with Pulled BBQ Jackfruit (page 63) sliders and Chick*n-Fried Portobello (page 66) or, do what I do, and eat it by the spoonful straight out of the pot.

8 cups (1.2 kg) corn kernels (10–12 ears) or use frozen

1 tbsp + 1 tsp (13 g) cornstarch

3 cups (709 ml) boiling water

1 tbsp (15 ml) grape-seed or canola oil

2 tbsp (13 g) diced shallot

2 tsp (10 ml) agave syrup

2½ tsp (13 g) sea salt

1 tsp coarse grind pepper (sometimes called butcher's grind)

Clean the corn and with a very sharp knife, trim the base of the cob so that it will stand flat on a cutting board when held vertically. Grab a clean kitchen towel and spread it over the cutting board. Bunch up the sides of the towel to form a wall. Holding the skinny end of the cob firmly, stand the cob in the center of your walled towel and carefully shave the kernels off the cob. This way keeps it minimally messy, but you may need to sweep up a few kernels that bounce onto the floor . . . or you can invite our dog Sydney over—she loves when I make this dish!

Remove 2 cups (350 g) of the corn kernels and purée them in the food processor. Add the remaining corn to the processor and pulse it to a coarse grind. You just want to break up the kernels.

Whisk the cornstarch into the boiling water and set aside until needed.

Heat the oil in a large pot over medium heat. When the oil is hot, add the shallot and the agave, and sauté for 2 minutes. Add all of the corn and continue to sauté, stirring regularly, for 3 minutes. Add the salt, pepper and the cornstarch-water mixture.

Bring the mixture to a very soft boil, stirring regularly with a wooden spoon. Reduce the heat to low and simmer the corn for 12 to 15 minutes or until the mixture thickens. Stir regularly.

Grab yourself a spoon. Remember, taste testing is a formal part of the cooking process!

BBQ Corn with Ginger-Agave Glaze

One of our definitions of summer includes fresh corn on the cob. Grab some cobs of your own and kick them up a notch with this tangy ginger-agave glaze.

¾ cup (177 ml) apple cider vinegar

¼ cup (60 ml) organic ketchup

¼ cup (60 ml) agave syrup

1½ tsp (22 g) minced ginger

1 large clove garlic, minced

¾ tsp hot sauce (we use habanero hot sauce)

¼ tsp sea salt

6 ears corn, shucked

2 tbsp (30 ml) corn or canola oil

2 tsp (10 g) sea salt

Prepare the glaze by combining the vinegar, ketchup, agave, ginger, garlic, hot sauce and salt in a saucepot over medium heat. Bring it to a very light boil and cook for 20 minutes or until the glaze has thickened and thickly coats the back of a spoon. Adjust the heat as necessary to maintain a very light boil and stir regularly. Remove from the heat and set the glaze aside until needed.

Preheat the grill to medium heat. Brush the cleaned corn cobs with the oil and sprinkle with the salt. Place the cobs on the grill and cook for 5 to 6 minutes per side or until the corn is lightly browned. Using tongs, turn the cobs regularly to ensure even browning.

Once the corn is lightly browned, brush on a thick layer of glaze and return the cobs to the grill. Grill for an additional 2 minutes per side. Brush with a bit more glaze, and serve with a side of napkins.

Perfect Quinoa

Yup, the name says it all! Rinsing the quinoa removes its natural coating of saponin that can often taste bitter when cooked. Toasting the quinoa adds a layer of nuttiness that'll take this complete protein to brand new heights.

1 cup (170 g) quinoa

1½ cups (360 ml) water

½ tsp sea salt

Rinse the quinoa in a strainer for 60 seconds under warm running water. Drain and place the quinoa in a medium pot over low heat. Toast the quinoa for 5 to 6 minutes, stirring regularly with a wooden spoon until the quinoa is dry, lightly toasted and smelling a little nutty.

Add the water and the salt to the pot. Raise the heat to high and bring the water to a boil. Reduce the heat to low, cover the pot and cook for 14 minutes.

Remove the pot from the heat and let the quinoa rest uncovered and untouched for 12 minutes. At this point, the quinoa seeds will have sprouted little white tails and the water will have been completely absorbed.

After resting, fluff the quinoa with a fork and serve.

Chapter 3

ACE IN THE BOWL

Bold Bowls, Broths and Brews

Try 'em all—but be sure to whip up a batch of our Mushroom Barley Soup (page 96) and join me on a vegan visit to the smells and tastes of my grandmother's kitchen.

Mushroom Barley Soup

The smell of this soup takes me back to my grandmother's kitchen when I was a little boy. This soup is rich and thick and creamy and delicious!

. . . .

1½ tbsp (22 ml) olive oil

1 cup (148 g) chopped red onion

6 cups (450 g) sliced brown mushrooms

½ cup (100 g) pearl barley

2 tsp (2 g) minced fresh rosemary

1 tsp dried dill

1 tsp smoked paprika

1 tsp sea salt

½ tsp freshly ground black pepper

2 tbsp (30 g) vegan butter

2 tbsp (16 g) flour

4 cups (946 ml) vegetable stock

½ cup (120 ml) Cashew Sour Cream (page 140)

¼ cup (60 ml) dry sherry

3 tbsp (8 g) chopped fresh parsley

1 tbsp (15 ml) tamari or soy sauce

Heat the oil in a soup pot over medium heat. When hot, add the onion and sauté for 4 to 5 minutes until translucent. Add the mushrooms and continue to sauté for 12 to 14 minutes until tender. Add the barley, rosemary, dill, paprika, salt and pepper. Mix together well and continue to sauté for 5 minutes.

In a small pan over medium-low heat, make a roux by whisking the butter and flour together. Whisk constantly for 2 to 3 minutes, until the mixture is golden and smells a bit nutty. Add the roux and the stock to the soup pot.

Bring the soup to a boil, then reduce the heat, maintaining a soft boil for 20 to 30 minutes or until the barley is puffed and tender.

Whisk in the Cashew Sour Cream, sherry, parsley and tamari. Continue to cook the soup for 10 minutes.

Serve the soup with a teaspoon of Cashew Sour Cream and a sprinkle of fresh parsley atop each bowl.

North African Peanut Soup

I'm so grateful that I don't have a peanut allergy, 'cause my life wouldn't be the same without this soup in it. This was one of the first soups I developed, and it's still one of the most asked for.

. . . .

2 tbsp (30 ml) peanut or canola oil

2 cups (300 g) chopped sweet onion

1 tbsp (15 g) minced ginger

¼ tsp cayenne pepper

2 cups (265 g) cubed sweet potato

1 cup (150 g) cubed carrot

4 cups (946 ml) vegetable stock

2 tbsp (30 g) tomato paste whisked with 1 cup (240 ml) water

1 cup (180 g) peanut butter

2 tbsp (24 g) evaporated cane sugar

3 tbsp (10 g) chopped chives, for garnish

Heat the oil in a soup pot over medium heat. When hot, add the chopped onion and sauté for approximately 5 minutes, until the onion is translucent. Add the ginger and cayenne pepper and continue to sauté, stirring constantly, for 1 minute.

Add the sweet potato and carrots and continue to sauté, stirring often, for 5 minutes. Add the stock, bring the soup to a boil and reduce the heat to low. Simmer for 20 to 30 minutes or until the sweet potato and carrots are fork tender.

Remove the soup from the heat and stir in the tomato paste mixture, peanut butter and sugar. Stir for 4 to 5 minutes until the peanut butter has melted and is completely incorporated.

Purée the soup in batches in your blender until it is velvety smooth. Return the soup to a clean pot and keep warm over low heat.

Garnish the soup with chopped chives.

This soup will thicken if refrigerated. Reheat the soup over low heat, adding a bit of stock or water to reach your desired consistency.

Curry Coconut Lentil Soup

Fragrant. Thick. Creamy. Each spoonful is a mini explosion of flavor in your mouth. And then there's that warm feeling that stays in the back of your throat. Serious, serious yum!

. . . .

1 tbsp (14 g) coconut oil

1 cup (130 g) diced sweet onion

2 small cloves garlic, minced

1 tbsp (15 g) minced ginger

2 tbsp (30 g) tomato paste

1½ tbsp (12 g) curry powder (we use a medium-heat curry powder at YamChops)

1 tsp garam masala

½ tsp red chili flakes

⅛ tsp cayenne pepper

4 cups (946 ml) vegetable stock

1 (13.5-oz [400-ml]) can coconut milk

2 medium tomatoes, seeded and diced

1½ cups (300 g) red lentils, rinsed

½ (210-g) block extra firm tofu, cut into ¼-inch (6-mm) cubes (see note)

1 cup (40 g) chopped baby spinach

Toasted coconut, for serving

Chopped green onions, for serving

Heat the oil in a soup pot over medium heat. When hot, add the onion and sauté for 3 minutes until the onion is just starting to soften. Add the garlic and ginger and continue to sauté for 2 minutes.

Add the tomato paste, curry powder, garam masala, chili flakes and cayenne pepper and continue to cook for 2 minutes, stirring constantly. Add the stock, milk, tomatoes and lentils to the pot. Bring the soup to a light boil, stirring regularly. Reduce the heat to low and simmer the soup for approximately 30 minutes or until the lentils are tender. You do not want this soup to boil.

Add the cubed tofu and chopped spinach, and continue to simmer for 5 minutes.

We like to serve this soup garnished with lightly toasted coconut and a sprinkle of chopped green onions.

This soup will thicken if refrigerated. Reheat the soup over low heat adding a bit of stock or water to reach your desired consistency.

Note: Always search out non-GMO tofu for tofu recipes.

Black Bean Soup

This is one of the original soups that I created during my ad agency days for our client, The Soup Bar. Yes, our agency certainly did redefine the phrase full service. This recipe has been updated a couple of times over the years, but all-in-all it has stayed true to its roots.

• •

1 tbsp (15 ml) olive oil

1 cup (148 g) chopped red onion

3 small cloves garlic, chopped

½ cup (75 g) chopped carrot

½ cup (110 g) chopped celery

¼ cup (50 g) chopped fennel

½ tsp ground cumin

½ tsp ground coriander

4 cups (946 ml) vegetable stock

½ cup (120 ml) fresh orange juice

1 (19-oz [540-ml]) can black beans, rinsed

⅛ tsp red chili flakes

¼ tsp salt

¼ tsp freshly ground black pepper

Mango Salsa (page 149), for serving

Heat the oil in a soup pot over medium heat. When hot, add the onion, garlic, carrot, celery and fennel. Sauté for approximately 8 minutes, until the vegetables are very fragrant and just beginning to soften. Add the cumin and coriander and continue to sauté, stirring constantly, for 1 minute.

Add the stock, orange juice, black beans, chili flakes, salt and pepper. Bring the soup to a boil and reduce the heat to medium-low. Cover the pot and simmer for 20 to 25 minutes or until the vegetables are tender.

Transfer the soup to a blender in batches and blend until smooth. Return the soup to a clean pot and keep it warm over low heat.

Serve the black bean soup in a shallow bowl with 1 tablespoon (13 g) of Mango Salsa (page 149) in the center of the bowl.

This soup will thicken if refrigerated. Reheat the soup over low heat adding a bit of stock or water to reach your desired consistency.

Hot and Sour Soup

This is one of our most popular soups on the counter. Our take on Hot and Sour veers away from the typical vinegary, black peppery, glumpy (yes, that's a cooking term!) soups found at most Asian restaurants and instead features lemony-limey, red curry, coconutty flavors in a veggie-packed broth.

. . . .

4 cups (946 ml) vegetable stock

2 cups (480 ml) water

1 stalk fresh lemongrass (inner white and light green parts only)

1 fresh lime, juiced

2 tsp (10 g) Thai red curry paste

2 small cloves garlic, minced

1 red pepper, cleaned

8 to 12 shiitake mushrooms, stems removed

8 to 12 cherry tomatoes

4 baby bok choy or 1 full-size bok choy

2 tbsp (30 ml) tamari or soy sauce

1 (416-g) block extra firm tofu, cut into ¼-inch (6-mm) cubes (see note)

2 tbsp (24 g) evaporated cane sugar

1 (14-oz [400-ml]) can coconut milk

2 tbsp (5 g) chopped fresh Thai basil, or regular basil

Large pinch cayenne pepper

1 tsp cornstarch mixed with 1 tbsp (15 ml) water

2 finely chopped green onions (white and light green part only)

Heat the stock and water over medium-high heat in a soup pot.

Trim the tough top and bottom of the lemongrass stalk. Cut the stalk into ½-inch (13-mm) pieces and remove the tough outer skin. Place only the white and light green part of the lemongrass into a high-speed blender. Add the lime juice, curry paste, garlic and ½ cup (120 ml) of the soup stock. Blend on high until smooth. There should only be very, very tiny pieces of the lemongrass remaining.

Add the lemongrass mixture to the soup pot and bring the soup base to a boil. Reduce the heat to maintain a low boil and continue cooking for 10 minutes.

Slice the red peppers into ⅛-inch (3-mm) strips and the mushroom caps into ¼-inch (6-mm) strips, and add to the pot. Halve the cherry tomatoes and add them to the pot. Stem the baby bok choy and remove the tough outer leaves. Chop the baby bok choy in ¾-inch (19-mm) pieces and add it to the pot.

Stir and continue to cook at a low boil for an additional 10 minutes.

Reduce the heat to simmer and add the tamari, tofu, sugar, coconut milk, basil and cayenne pepper. Stir well.

Prepare a slurry by whisking the cornstarch and water together with a fork. Slowly add the slurry to the soup, mixing well so that it doesn't clump. Let the soup continue to cook for 3 or 4 minutes or until it has thickened. Serve topped with the green onions.

Note: Always search out non-GMO tofu for tofu recipes.

Lemon Lentil Soup

You never know when a nearly empty fridge and an equally nearly empty cupboard will produce a keeper. We had just moved to our new house and this soup came about from the meager offerings we had in the fridge, cupboard and herb garden. As good as this soup is, it didn't make unpacking any less painful.

. . . .

1 tbsp (15 ml) olive oil

¾ cup (115 g) chopped sweet onion

3 small cloves garlic, chopped

½ tsp sea salt

¾ cup (60 g) chopped carrots

1½ tsp (1 g) dried oregano

1 bay leaf

1½ tsp (2 g) chopped fresh rosemary

½ tsp freshly ground black pepper

⅛ tsp red chili flakes

6 cups (1.4 L) vegetable stock

1 cup (200 g) red lentils, rinsed

Zest and juice of 1 lemon

1 tbsp (3 g) chopped fresh dill, for garnish

Heat the oil in a soup pot over medium heat. When hot, add the onion and sauté for approximately 5 minutes until translucent. Add the garlic and salt and continue to sauté for 1 minute. Add the carrots, oregano, bay leaf, rosemary, pepper and chili flakes and continue to sauté, stirring regularly, for 4 minutes.

Add the stock and lentils and bring the soup to a boil. Reduce the heat to low and simmer for 30 minutes or until the lentils are soft, but still retain a little bit of bite.

Remove the bay leaf and purée the soup in batches in a blender until it is smooth. Return the soup to a clean pot, stir in the lemon zest and juice, and keep warm over low heat.

Garnish the soup with the dill.

This soup will thicken if refrigerated. Reheat the soup over low heat adding a bit of stock or water to reach your desired consistency.

Margot-Strone with White Beans

Yes, this is a thick and hearty minestrone soup. Yes, it's called Margot-Strone, and that's because I created this as a special request for my son-in-law's sister who loved it. She made me promise that if I ever wrote a cookbook that I would name this soup Margot-Strone! A promise is a promise!

. . . .

3 tbsp (45 ml) olive oil

1 cup (150 g) sweet onion cut in ¼-inch (6-mm) dice

3 small cloves garlic, minced

5 cups (1.2 L) vegetable stock

2 cups (360 g) peeled russet potato cut in ½-inch (13-mm) cubes

1 cup (161 g) tomato cut in ½-inch (13-mm) cubes

1 cup (270 g) zucchini cut in ¼-inch (6-mm) half moons

2 cups (300 g) green beans cut in 1-inch (25-mm) pieces

1 cup (180 g) carrots cut in ¼-inch (6-mm) rounds

2 tbsp (5 g) chopped fresh oregano

1 (5-oz [142-g]) can tomato paste

¼ cup (5 g) chopped fresh parsley

¼ cup (5 g) chopped fresh basil

½ tsp sea salt

½ tsp freshly ground pepper

1 (19-oz [540-g]) can white beans, rinsed

1 cup (100 g) elbow macaroni or baby pasta shells

Heat the oil in a soup pot over medium heat. When hot, add the onion and sauté for approximately 5 minutes until translucent. Add the garlic and continue to sauté for 1 minute. Add the stock, potatoes, tomatoes, zucchini, beans, carrots and oregano and stir together well. Increase the heat to high and bring to a boil. Once boiling, reduce the heat to low, cover the pot and simmer for 20 minutes or until the veggies are tender but still crunchy.

Remove 1 cup (240 ml) of the broth to a bowl and whisk in the tomato paste, parsley, basil, salt and pepper. Add it back to the pot along with the white beans and pasta. Raise the heat to medium, cover the pot and cook until the pasta is tender, about 11 minutes.

This is a very thick (and filling) soup. You can thin it with additional stock or water if you'd prefer it thinner.

Better yet, grab a wedge of crusty bread, fill a big bowl with soup and don't let anyone disturb you.

Red-Hot Red Tomato Soup

This ain't no soup out of a can. Kicked up with the fragrance of cinnamon and coriander, and punched up with ginger and cayenne, this soup and a grilled cheeze sandwich are kinda like the perfect couple!

. . . .

1½ tbsp (22 ml) grape-seed or canola oil

¾ cup (115 g) diced sweet onion

¾ cup (130 g) chopped red pepper

3 tbsp (45 g) minced ginger

2 large cloves garlic, chopped

2 cups (480 ml) vegetable stock

4 cups (645 g) diced tomatoes

1 tsp ground coriander

¼ tsp cinnamon

¼ tsp cayenne

2 tbsp (30 ml) tomato paste

2 cups (480 ml) fresh orange juice

1½ tsp (8 g) sea salt

Cashew Sour Cream (page 140), for serving

Minced chives, for serving

Heat the oil in a soup pot over medium heat. When hot, add the onion, red pepper, ginger and garlic, and sauté for 6 to 7 minutes or until the veggies have softened.

Add the stock, tomatoes, coriander, cinnamon and cayenne and stir well. Cook, stirring regularly, for 15 minutes. You're after a very gentle boil when cooking this soup. You don't want a full rolling boil.

Add the tomato paste, orange juice and salt and stir well. Continue to cook, stirring regularly, for an additional 15 minutes.

Reduce the heat to low and simmer the soup for an additional 15 minutes.

Carefully blend the soup in batches in your blender until smooth.

We like to serve this soup with a tablespoon (15 ml) of Cashew Sour Cream in the center of the bowl and a sprinkling of minced chives over top.

Cranberry and Wild Rice Soup

An earthy soup that combines the nuttiness of wild rice with the tang of dried cranberries in a wonderfully rich broth. The elevated flavors of this soup make it the perfect opener to any holiday meal.

3 tbsp (45 g) vegan butter

1 tbsp (15 ml) olive oil

½ cup (75 g) diced sweet onion

⅓ cup (75 g) diced celery

⅓ cup (45 g) diced carrot

1 tsp minced fresh sage

3 tbsp (24 g) unbleached all-purpose flour

4 cups (946 ml) vegetable stock

1½ cups (266 g) cooked wild rice (see note)

½ cup (60 g) dried cranberries

2 tbsp (30 ml) dry sherry

1 cup (240 ml) almond milk

1 tsp sea salt

½ tsp freshly ground black pepper

Lemon, for serving

Melt the butter and olive oil in a Dutch oven or soup pot over medium heat. Add the onion, celery and carrot, and cook, stirring occasionally, for 10 minutes, or until the carrot is crisp tender. Add the sage and continue to cook for 2 minutes.

Sprinkle the flour over the sautéing veggies. Gradually add the stock, whisking to prevent lumps. Increase the heat to medium-high and continue to cook, stirring regularly, for 5 to 7 minutes or until the soup has thickened. Stir in the cooked wild rice and the cranberries. Reduce the heat to low, cover the pot and simmer for 15 minutes.

Stir in the sherry, almond milk, salt and pepper. Simmer the soup uncovered for 5 minutes.

Serve this soup with a wedge of lemon on the side.

Note: To prepare the wild rice, rinse ½ cup (72 g) of wild rice under cold water for 30 seconds and drain in a sieve. Add the rice, 2 cups (240 ml) of water and ½ teaspoon of sea salt to a pot over medium-high heat. Once the water begins to boil, reduce the heat to low, cover the pot and simmer for 45 to 50 minutes or until the wild rice kernels have opened and are al dente. Let the rice drain in a sieve until needed.

Tortilla Soup

Although the ingredient list is a bit lengthy, this soup comes together really quickly. It's thick and rich, and it brings the warmth of the Mexican sun right to your table. Top the soup bowls with cubed avocado, crispy tortilla strips, sliced green onions and a tablespoon (15 ml) of Cashew Sour Cream (page 140) for the perfect finish.

. . . .

2 tbsp (30 ml) olive oil

½ medium sweet onion, cut into ½-inch (13-mm) slices

3 small cloves garlic, chopped

1 medium (25 g) jalapeño pepper, seeded and cut into ½-inch (13-mm) slices

1 (28-oz [806-ml]) can fire-roasted diced tomatoes

½ tsp chipotle chili powder

¼ tsp Mexican chili powder

¼ tsp ground cumin

¼ tsp Mexican oregano

1 tbsp (15 ml) agave syrup

1 tsp sherry vinegar

6 cups (1.4 L) vegetable stock

3 (6-inch [152-mm]) soft corn tortillas (cut into 1-inch [25-mm] pieces)

1 cup (146 g) corn kernels, fresh or frozen

1 cup (250 g) black beans, rinsed

2 cups (480 ml) unsweetened almond or other plant-based milk

1 cup (185 g) cooked quinoa

3 tbsp (45 ml) lime juice

1 tsp salt

Avocado, for serving

Tortilla strips, for serving

Green onions, for serving

Cashew Sour Cream (page 140), for serving

Heat the oil in a soup pot over medium heat. When hot, add the onion and sauté for approximately 10 minutes until the onion is just starting to brown. Add the garlic and jalapeño pepper, and continue to sauté for 3 minutes.

Add the tomatoes, chili powders, cumin, oregano, agave, vinegar, stock, tortillas, corn and beans to the pot. Stir together well. Raise the heat and bring the soup to a boil, then reduce the heat to low and simmer the soup for 20 minutes.

Add the almond milk, quinoa, lime juice and salt to the pot. Stir together well. Continue to simmer the soup for an additional 10 minutes.

Carefully purée the soup in batches in your blender until smooth and creamy. Taste and adjust seasoning if necessary.

Serve topped with cubed avocado, crispy tortilla strips, sliced green onions and a spoonful of Cashew Sour Cream.

Kale Caesar! Bowl

Our number one-selling bowl! If the creator of the Caesar Salad, Caesar Cardini, were vegan, this is the salad he would have come up with!

. . . .

Caesar Dressing (page 120)

Green kale, enough to fill 6 salad bowls

¾ cup (115 g) diced red onion

¾ cup (40 g) thinly sliced sun-dried tomatoes (not packed in oil)

Coconut Ba-con (page 72)

Hemp Parm (page 157)

Prepare the dressing.

Remove the center stems of the kale and tear the leaves into bite-size pieces and place in a large bowl. Massage the kale between your fingers for a few minutes to get rid of its bitterness.

Remove the dressing from the refrigerator. Mix the dressing well and add ⅓ to ½ cup (80 to 120 ml) of dressing to the bowl. Mix well. You want the kale to be evenly coated in the dressing.

Divide the kale into 6 salad bowls. Sprinkle 2 tablespoons (25 g) of red onion over the top of each bowl followed by 2 tablespoons (19 g) of the sun-dried tomatoes.

Sprinkle generously with Coconut Ba-con and Hemp Parm.

Dragon Bowl

Nine months after we opened YamChops' doors, we received an email from CBC's *Dragons' Den*, Canada's number one investment reality TV show. They were inviting us to appear on the show! Following our appearance on *Dragons' Den*, we created this bowl of deliciousness in the Dragons' honor.

· ·

Buddha Dressing

¼ cup (60 ml) grape-seed or canola oil

1 cup (45 g) nutritional yeast

⅜ cup (88 ml) apple cider vinegar

⅓ cup (80 ml) tamari or soy sauce (use gluten-free tamari to make this dish gluten-free)

⅓ cup (60 g) organic cane sugar or maple syrup

1 large clove garlic, peeled and roughly chopped

1 tsp sea salt

¾ tsp ginger powder

Bowl

1 cup (185 g) long grain brown rice

6 cups (1.4 L) water

1 tsp sea salt

Freshly ground pepper

1 small sweet potato

1 tbsp (15 ml) olive oil

1 green zucchini

3 cups (300 g) green cabbage

1 cup (100 g) purple cabbage

1 large or 2 small red or golden beets, peeled

1 large or 2 small carrots, peeled

2 tbsp (30 g) roasted unsalted pepitas

To make the dressing, add the oil, yeast, vinegar, tamari, sugar, garlic, salt and ginger powder to a high-speed blender and blend until smooth, scraping down the sides of the blender a couple of times. Place the dressing in a bowl, cover with plastic wrap and refrigerate until needed.

Preheat the oven to 400°F (204°C) and start a grill or grill pan going on medium-high heat.

To prepare the brown rice, bring the water to a boil over high heat. Add 1 teaspoon of sea salt. Rinse the rice in a sieve under cold water for 1 minute. Add the rice to the boiling water and stir once. Boil, uncovered, for 55 minutes, until al dente. Turn off the heat, drain the rice in a sieve for 15 seconds and return to the pot. Cover the pot and let rice rest for 15 minutes off the heat.

To prepare the sweet potato, peel and cut into ½-inch (13-mm) cubes. Place the cubed sweet potato in a bowl, add the olive oil and a sprinkle of sea salt and pepper. Toss well to coat and place the cubes on a parchment paper lined baking sheet. Place in the preheated oven and bake for approximately 20 minutes, until golden and just beginning to brown. Mix every 5 minutes or so. When the sweet potatoes are ready, remove from the oven and set aside to cool.

To prepare the zucchini, remove the ends and with a mandoline or sharp knife, slice into ⅛-inch (3-mm)-thick planks. Brush both sides with olive oil and sprinkle with sea salt and pepper. Grill until nicely grill marked on both sides, approximately 2 minutes per side. When the zucchini are ready, remove from the grill, cut into ½-inch (13-mm) squares and set aside to cool.

To prepare the veggies, shred the cabbages and grate the beets and carrots. If you're using red beets, cover the cutting board with plastic wrap and wear plastic gloves to avoid staining. Keep all vegetables separate until you're ready to serve.

Time to build the bowls! Divide the grated cabbage among four bowls. Place one-fourth of the brown rice in the center of the bowl. Arrange the grated beets, grated carrots, grilled zucchini and roasted sweet potatoes around the mound of brown rice. Sprinkle the pepitas over each bowl.

Mix the dressing well and drizzle 2 generous tablespoons (30 ml) over each bowl.

Cumin-Lime, Black Bean and Quinoa Bowl

You know the feeling when everything just melds together in perfect harmony? This is that feeling. Warming cumin, tart lime and sweet maple syrup combine to elevate the flavor of everything else in this bowl of goodness.

• •

1½ cups (200 g) sweet potato peeled and cut in ½-inch (13-mm) cubes

1 tbsp (15 ml) olive oil

Sea salt

Freshly ground pepper

Spring mix

1½ cups (277 g) cooked quinoa

1½ cups (90 g) canned black beans, rinsed well

1½ cups (75 g) grated carrot

Cumin-Lime Dressing
⅛ cup (80 ml) fresh lime juice

2 tbsp (30 ml) maple syrup

2 tbsp (10 g) grated carrot

2 small cloves garlic, minced

2 tsp (5 g) ground cumin

1 tsp sea salt

¼ cup (60 ml) olive oil

Preheat the oven to 400°F (204°C).

Place the sweet potato in a bowl, add oil and sprinkle sea salt and freshly ground pepper. Toss well to coat and place the cubes on a parchment paper lined baking sheet. Place in the preheated oven and bake for approximately 20 minutes until golden and just beginning to brown. Mix every 5 minutes or so. When the sweet potatoes are ready, remove from the oven and set aside to cool.

To make the dressing, add the lime juice, syrup, carrot, garlic, cumin and salt to a blender and blend until smooth. With the blender running on low, slowly drizzle in the olive oil in a steady stream. Place the dressing in a bowl, cover with plastic wrap and refrigerate until needed.

Start with a base of spring mix in 6 shallow bowls. Divide the quinoa, black beans, carrot and potato among the bowls.

Mix the dressing well and drizzle 2 generous tablespoons (30 ml) over each bowl.

Mediterranean Bowl

This is our vegan version of a Greek Salad done the YamChops way. Take things up a notch or two by whipping up a batch of our Feta Cheeze (page 88) and crumbling it over your bowls. By the way, the pickled red onions from this recipe also make a great burger or salad topping.

. . . .

Pickled Red Onions

2 medium red onions, thinly sliced in half moons

4 small cloves garlic, minced

¾ cup (177 ml) white wine vinegar

½ cup (120 ml) water

¼ cup (60 ml) olive oil

1 tbsp + 1 tsp (20 ml) fresh lemon juice

1 tbsp + 1 tsp (2 g) dried oregano

1 tbsp + 1 tsp (16 g) evaporated cane sugar

1 tbsp (15 g) sea salt

2 tsp (4 g) coarse grind pepper (sometimes called butcher's grind)

Mediterranean Dressing

1 cup (220 g) vegan mayo

½ cup (120 ml) brine (from the pickled red onions)

¼ cup (60 ml) olive oil

1 tsp dried oregano

Bowl

2 heads romaine lettuce, chopped into 1-inch (25-mm) pieces

3 cups (555 g) cooked quinoa

1 red pepper, thinly sliced

2 carrots, peeled and grated

1 (19-oz [540-ml]) can white beans, rinsed

18 black olives

To prepare the pickled red onions, place the onions and garlic in a medium bowl. In a separate bowl, whisk together the vinegar, water, oil, lemon juice, oregano, sugar, salt and pepper to make your brine. Add the brine to the onions and mix together well. Allow the onions to marinate for a minimum of 1 hour (overnight is better). Tightly covered in the refrigerator, the onions will keep for 2 weeks.

To prepare the dressing, whisk together the mayo, brine, oil and oregano, cover with plastic wrap and place in the refrigerator until needed.

To make the bowls, divide the romaine lettuce among 6 salad bowls. Top each bowl with quinoa, then thinly sliced red pepper and grated carrots. Add a small handful of white beans to each bowl along with 3 black olives.

Drizzle 3 tablespoons (45 ml) of dressing over each bowl and top with a forkful of pickled onions.

Chapter 4

IT'S CRUNCH TIME

Remarkable Salads, Slaws and Dips

From smooth and creamy Roasted Butternut Squash Hummus (page 127) to crisp and crunchy Agave-Lime Slaw (page 130), these versatile recipes will send your palate on a taste and texture vacation.

Caesar Dressing

We just can't make enough of this dressing! Of course we use this dressing on our Kale Caesar! Bowl (page 110), and it's also great as a dip for fresh-cut veggies or as the creaminess in creamy mashed potatoes or as a squeeze over grilled veggies . . .

Makes approximately 1 ½ cups (360 ml)

1¼ cups (275 g) vegan mayo

2 tbsp (30 ml) white vinegar

1 tbsp (5 g) surfine capers, rinsed (see note)

2 tsp (2 g) nutritional yeast

2 tsp (10 ml) fresh lemon juice

2 tsp (10 ml) grainy Dijon mustard

½ tsp salt

¼ tsp freshly ground black pepper

Add all of the dressing ingredients to a bowl and whisk together until fully mixed. Covered and refrigerated, this dressing will last for 2 weeks.

Note: Surfine capers are pickled young to retain their flavor and texture. They are about the size of a small pea. If you can only find the larger capote, capucine, fine or grusas capers, that's okay—just be sure to cut them into pea-size pieces.

Basil Dressing

We love this fresh basil dressing! We use it to top our vegan caprese salad, as a dressing for our roasted corn, tomato and quinoa salad, as a pesto between layers of grilled zucchini . . . and sometimes we just slather it on thick slices of summer heirloom tomatoes and snack in the kitchen.

Makes approximately 1 cup (240 ml)

½ cup (18 g) chopped packed fresh basil

6 tbsp (90 ml) fresh lemon juice

3 tbsp (35 g) evaporated cane sugar

2 tbsp (30 ml) tamari or soy sauce

2 small cloves garlic, chopped

½ tsp coarse grind pepper (sometimes called butcher's grind)

⅔ cup (158 ml) olive oil

Place the basil, lemon juice, sugar, tamari, garlic and pepper in a blender. Pulse the mixture 3 or 4 times to combine.

With the processor running on low, slowly pour in the olive oil in a steady stream until the dressing is emulsified.

Store in a covered jar in the refrigerator and shake well before using.

Ranch Dressing

We use this dressing to tone down the heat on our Buffalo Chick*n wrap. It also makes a really nice dip for fresh-cut veggies, deep-fried pickles, breaded cauliflower and on our Fishless Tacos (page 45).

Makes approximately 1 cup (240 ml)

½ cup (110 g) vegan mayo
½ lemon, juiced
1½ tbsp (22 ml) rice vinegar
1½ tbsp (5 g) nutritional yeast
1½ tbsp (4 g) minced fresh dill
1 tbsp (6 g) minced shallot
2 tsp (10 ml) agave syrup

Add all of the ingredients to a bowl and whisk well to combine.

Store covered in the refrigerator for up to 2 weeks.

Miso-Sesame Dressing

This lively dressing works beautifully in place of our Szechuan Dressing on our Szechuan Noodle Salad (page 122), and it doubles as a sauce for your next stir fry.

Makes approximately 1 cup (240 ml)

½ cup (120 ml) rice vinegar
¼ cup + 2 tbsp (100 g) white miso
8 small cloves garlic, minced
3 tbsp (45 g) sambal oelek
3 tbsp (45 ml) sesame oil
3 tbsp (45 ml) agave syrup
2 tbsp (5 g) chopped fresh basil
1 tbsp (3 g) chopped fresh parsley

Place all of the ingredients into a food processor and pulse a half-dozen times or so to fully mix. Pour the dressing into a saucepot set over medium heat and cook, stirring often, until it reaches a soft boil. Maintain a soft boil and cook for 5 minutes to slightly thicken the dressing.

Covered tightly, this dressing lasts for 1 week in the refrigerator.

Szechuan Noodle Salad

This scrumptious cold noodle bowl is equally scrumptious with our Miso-Sesame Dressing (page 121). We use a gluten-free buckwheat soba noodle at YamChops, but you can certainly substitute with any thin, long noodle.

1 lb (453 g) buckwheat soba noodles

2 tsp (10 ml) sesame oil

1½ cups (75 g) carrot, grated

1 large red pepper, thinly sliced

½ medium English cucumber, seeded and thinly sliced

4 green onions, thinly sliced

¼ cup (40 g) roasted unsalted cashews, roughly chopped

Dressing

2 tbsp (30 ml) sesame oil

1½ tsp (1 g) dried red chili flakes

3 small cloves garlic, minced

1 cup (240 ml) water

½ cup (120 ml) gluten-free tamari or soy sauce

5 tbsp (75 ml) agave syrup

2 tbsp (30 ml) rice vinegar

2 tsp (6 g) arrowroot or cornstarch mixed with 2 tbsp (30 ml) water

¼ cup (60 ml) lime juice

2 tbsp (5 g) minced fresh basil

Bring a large pot of salted water to a boil and cook the noodles according to the package directions. When the noodles are ready, drain them in a colander and rinse them well under cold water. Drain the noodles again and then place them in a large bowl. Add the sesame oil and mix well to coat the noodles. Set aside until needed.

While the noodles are cooking, prepare the dressing. Heat the sesame oil in a large sauté pan over low heat. When the oil is hot, add the chili flakes and sauté for 1 minute. Add the minced garlic and continue to sauté for an additional minute. Raise the heat to medium and add the water, tamari, agave and rice vinegar. Continue to cook, stirring regularly, for 5 to 7 minutes or until the mixture just begins to gently boil.

Stir together the arrowroot and water to form a slurry. Whisk the slurry into the gently boiling mixture. Continue to cook for 3 to 4 minutes, whisking constantly, until the mixture has thickened slightly. Remove the mixture from the heat and whisk in the lime juice and the basil. Set aside to cool.

Place one-fourth of the noodles in the base of four salad bowls. Top the noodles with the carrot, red pepper, cucumber and green onion. Drizzle 2 to 3 tablespoons (30 to 45 ml) of the dressing over each of the bowls. Finish with a sprinkle of the roasted cashews.

Cashew-Chickpea Hummus

This hummus pairs beautifully with our Mango Tamarind Chutney (page 154) and it feels right at home on a cheeze platter, at a Middle Eastern feast and as a sandwich spread.

. . . .

¼ cup (60 ml) grape-seed or canola oil

10 thin slices fresh peeled ginger

⅛ cup (37 g) roasted unsalted cashews

1 (15-oz [420-g]) can chickpeas, rinsed

Juice of 1 lime

1 clove garlic, minced

1 tsp ground cumin

1 tsp ground coriander

½ tsp sea salt

½ tsp coarse grind pepper (sometimes called butcher's grind)

¼ tsp cayenne pepper

Large pinch cinnamon powder

Large pinch turmeric powder

2 tbsp (5 g) chopped fresh mint

2 tbsp (5 g) chopped fresh basil

Gently heat the oil in a small pot over medium-low heat. Add the ginger slices and let them gently bubble for 10 minutes. Maintain a low setting so that the ginger does not brown. Remove the pot from the heat and set aside to cool.

Add the cashews, ginger slices and oil to a food processor and pulse to coarsely chop them. Add the chickpeas to the processor along with the lime juice and garlic. Pulse to break up the chickpeas. Add the cumin, coriander, salt, pepper, cayenne pepper, cinnamon and turmeric to the processor, and pulse to mix everything together. Add the mint and basil, and pulse a few more times to incorporate the herbs into the hummus.

You're after a fairly thick hummus that still has some coarse chickpea pieces. You don't want to over-process this hummus.

Try this hummus in a wrap topped with Mango Tamarind Chutney (page 154), shredded lettuce, grated carrots and julienned cucumber. You'll be back for seconds!

Black Bean Hummus and Mango Mojo

Mound this hummus on a bed of slaw and top it with julienned red peppers, pepitas and a squeeze of Mango Mojo.

. . . .

1 (19-oz [540-ml]) can black beans

⅓ cup (50 g) pepitas

1 large clove garlic, minced

2 tbsp (30 ml) lime juice

2 tsp (7 g) minced chipotle in adobo

½ tsp sea salt

½ tsp ground cumin

½ tsp ground coriander

2 tbsp (5 g) chopped fresh basil

2 tbsp (30 ml) olive oil

Mango Mojo
1 ripe mango

3 tbsp (45 ml) fresh lime juice

1 small clove garlic, chopped

½ small jalapeño (with seeds)

½ tsp sea salt

1 tbsp (3 g) chopped fresh basil

Rinse and drain the black beans. Add the black beans to a food processor along with the pepitas and garlic. Pulse a half-dozen times to break up the black beans. Add the lime juice, chipotle in adobo, salt, cumin and coriander to the processor and pulse a few times to incorporate everything. Add the basil and the oil and pulse a few more times.

To make the mango mojo, peel and pit the mango. Add the mango flesh to the blender, along with the lime juice, garlic, jalapeño, salt and basil. Blend on high until smooth.

Top the hummus with a splash of the mango mojo.

Roasted Butternut Squash Hummus

This dip feels right at home on a cheeze platter, or slathered on a cracker, or heaped on a pita wedge, or as a sandwich spread . . . are you getting the picture?

2 cups (300 g) butternut squash, peeled and cut in ½-inch (13-mm) cubes

½ cup + 2 tbsp (150 ml) olive oil, divided

1 tsp sea salt

¼ tsp freshly ground pepper

3 cloves garlic, paper skin on

1 (15-oz [420-g]) can chickpeas, rinsed

1 tsp smoked paprika

1 tsp ground cumin

Large pinch cayenne pepper

2 tbsp (23 g) tahini

Juice of 1 lemon

1 tbsp (15 ml) maple syrup

Preheat the oven to 400°F (204°C).

Toss the butternut squash cubes in a bowl with the 2 tablespoons (30 ml) of oil, salt and pepper. Place the garlic cloves in a small square of aluminum foil and fold the foil into a packet. Spread the squash on a parchment paper lined–baking sheet and add the aluminum foil packet of garlic to the sheet. Roast until the cubes are tender and browned in quite a few spots. Mix them up from time to time on the baking sheet to ensure even browning.

Place the roasted butternut squash in a food processor. Unwrap the garlic packet and squeeze the softened garlic cloves out of their paper skins and into the processor. Add the rinsed chickpeas and pulse a few times just to get things broken up a bit. Add the paprika, cumin and cayenne, and pulse a few more times.

Finally, add ½ cup (120 ml) of oil, tahini, lemon juice and maple syrup and process until smoooooth!

3C Slaw

Our 3C Slaw fits the bill as a side slaw, a burger topping or a taco filling! It also holds really well, and that makes it a perfect picnic and BBQ potluck dish.

. . . .

1 cup (240 ml) water

¼ cup + 3 tbsp (100 ml) white wine vinegar

1 tbsp + ¼ tsp (16 g) sea salt, divided

2½ cups (375 g) raw corn kernels

2 tbsp (30 ml) olive oil

Pinch freshly ground black pepper

4½ cups (450 g) shredded cabbage, green, red or a combination

1½ cups (75 g) shredded carrot

1 medium red onion, thinly sliced into crescents

1 small Thai red or green chili, thinly sliced

1 cup (25 g) fresh parsley, finely chopped

⅓ cup (10 g) fresh mint leaves, finely chopped

Freshly ground pepper

Dressing
¼ cup (58 g) vegan mayo

2 tbsp (30 ml) lime juice

2 tsp (10 ml) Dijon mustard

2 tsp (7 g) chipotle in adobo, minced

1 small garlic clove, minced

Preheat the oven to 350°F (177°C).

Bring the water, vinegar and ¼ teaspoon of salt to a boil in a small pot. Boil for 60 seconds and then remove the pot from the heat. This is the brine.

Place the corn kernels in a bowl and mix in the oil and the remaining 1 tablespoon (15 g) of the salt. Spread the kernels on a parchment paper lined baking sheet and place the sheet in the preheated oven. Roast the corn, stirring often, for 12 to 15 minutes, until the kernels are golden and just starting to brown in a few spots. Remove from the oven and set aside to cool.

Mix the cabbage, carrot and red onion together in a large bowl. Pour the brine over the slaw and fold it all together. Let the slaw marinate for 30 minutes.

Prepare the dressing by whisking all of the dressing ingredients together in a bowl.

Once the slaw has marinated for 30 minutes, drain it well in a colander. Place the drained slaw in a bowl and add the chili, parsley and mint. Add the dressing and mix it all together.

Sprinkle with the remaining sea salt and freshly ground pepper and mix it all together once more.

Asian Pear, Daikon and Carrot Slaw

Makes approximately 2½ cups (852 g)

This slaw is the soulmate to our Thai Tofu Burgers (page 33). It's fresh and crunchy with just the right amount of sweet and heat.

· ·

1 cup (50 g) peeled grated carrot

1 cup (100 g) julienned daikon radish

1 large Asian pear, peeled, cored and julienned

3 tbsp (45 ml) rice vinegar

3 tbsp (45 ml) agave syrup

¼ tsp red pepper flakes

⅛ tsp white pepper

Combine the carrot, daikon and pear in a large bowl.

In a small bowl, whisk together the rice vinegar, agave, red pepper flakes and white pepper. Add the dressing to the slaw and mix together well. Allow the slaw to rest for 30 minutes for the flavors to meld before serving.

Agave-Lime Slaw

Okay, we'll admit it. We're slawoholics. We love the crunch and extra layer of flavor that they add to most anything! This slaw wonderfully pairs with our Pulled BBQ Jackfruit (page 63).

Makes approximately 2½ cups (852 g)

1 cup (100 g) shredded purple cabbage

1 cup (50 g) grated carrot

½ cup (50 g) shaved fennel

2 tbsp (30 ml) agave syrup

2 tbsp (30 ml) lime juice

½ tsp sea salt

Combine the cabbage, carrot and fennel in a large bowl.

In a small bowl, whisk together the agave, lime juice and salt. Pour the dressing over the slaw and, using your hands, toss it all together. Allow the slaw to rest for 30 minutes for the flavors to meld before serving.

Garlic Aioli

At YamChops, this tzatziki-style dressing tops our falafel and chick*n shawarma. We love it over grilled veggies, and it also adds a wonderful creaminess to mashed potatoes. One of our favorite uses of this aioli is as a sauce for our Chick*n Schnitzel (page 14).

Makes approximately 1½ cups (360 ml)

1½ cups (330 g) vegan mayo

4 large cloves garlic, chopped

3 tbsp (45 ml) water

2 tsp (1 g) dried parsley

½ tsp dried oregano

2 tsp (10 g) sea salt

Place all of the ingredients in a food processor or blender and blend well to combine.

Covered and refrigerated, this dressing lasts for 2 weeks.

Creamy Pasta Salad

One of the things we love to do at YamChops is to veganize some of our favorite dishes from our pre-vegan days. This is that! With its mild curry undertones, crispy veggies, fresh herbs and wonderful creamy consistency—we're certain it'll quickly become one of your favorites too! This pasta salad also holds really well, so keep it in mind for your next picnic or backyard BBQ!

1 cup (100 g) elbow macaroni or baby shells

1 tbsp (15 ml) olive oil

⅓ cup (60 g) fresh or frozen corn kernels (thawed if frozen)

⅓ cup (15 g) diced carrot

2 tbsp (25 g) diced celery

2 tbsp (22 g) diced red pepper

2 tbsp (6 g) minced green onion

2 tsp (5 g) minced fresh parsley

2 tsp (5 g) minced fresh dill

½ cup (110 g) vegan mayo

1 tbsp (15 ml) lemon juice

1 tbsp (15 ml) maple syrup

2 tsp (5 g) mild curry powder

2 tsp (5 g) Aleppo pepper or ancho chili powder

1 tsp sea salt

¼ tsp black pepper

⅛ tsp cayenne pepper

Cook the pasta in a large pot of boiling water for 9 minutes or until al dente. Drain the pasta and add it to a large bowl. Add the oil and stir together to keep the pasta from sticking. Add the corn, carrot, celery, red pepper, green onion, parsley and dill to the bowl and mix everything together.

In a separate bowl whisk together the mayo, lemon juice, maple syrup, curry powder, Aleppo pepper, salt, black pepper and cayenne pepper.

Add the dressing to the pasta and fold everything together with a spatula. Cover and refrigerate the pasta salad for 30 minutes before serving to allow the flavors to meld.

Fusion Potato Salad

This fusion came together one afternoon when my daughter Jessie and I were free-styling in the kitchen. It's definitely a unique collection of ingredients that you wouldn't necessarily think of putting together in the same bowl, but they really do fuse together beautifully.

· ·

2 lb (900 g) Yukon Gold potatoes, cut into 1 inch (25 mm) cubes

2 tbsp (30 ml) olive oil

1 cup (150 g) diced sweet onion

2 large cloves garlic, minced

1 cup (150 g) fresh or frozen corn kernels, thawed if frozen

½ cup (75 g) fresh or frozen peas

1 cup (220 g) vegan mayo

2 tbsp (30 ml) lemon juice

1 tbsp (15 ml) vegan Worcestershire sauce

2 tsp (10 g) sambal oelek

1 tsp sesame oil

1 tsp wasabi powder mixed with 2 tsp (10 ml) water

1 tsp ground ginger

½ tsp ground turmeric

3 tbsp (8 g) chopped fresh basil

½ tsp sea salt

½ tsp coarse grind pepper (sometimes called butcher's grind)

Bring a large pot of salted water to a boil and cook the potatoes for 10 minutes or until they can easily be pierced with a skewer. Drain the potatoes in a colander and run them under cold water to halt the cooking process.

Add the olive oil to a skillet set over medium heat. Once hot, add the onions and sauté for 5 minutes or until they are translucent. Add the garlic and sauté an additional minute. Add the corn and peas, and sauté for an additional 5 minutes.

Place the potatoes and the onion mixture in a large bowl. In a separate bowl, whisk together the mayo, lemon juice, Worcestershire, sambal oelek, sesame oil, wasabi paste, ginger and turmeric. Add the dressing and the basil to the bowl and fold everything together with a spatula. Let the salad rest for 30 minutes before serving for the flavors to meld.

Season with salt and pepper.

Lemon-Lime Quinoa and Roasted Corn

You can use fresh corn kernels shaved directly off the cob or thawed frozen corn kernels, but the best way is to take the time to roast the corn to bring out its natural sweetness. This is a wonderful summery salad that's perfect all year long.

. . . .

1 cup (150 g) corn kernels, thawed if frozen

2 tbsp (30 ml) olive oil

1 tsp sea salt, plus more for seasoning corn

Coarse black pepper

2 cups (370 g) cooked quinoa

3 tbsp (38 g) diced red pepper

3 tbsp (38 g) diced green pepper

2 tbsp (25 g) minced jalapeño pepper

2 tbsp (5 g) chopped fresh basil

2 tbsp (6 g) minced green onion

2 tbsp + 2 tsp (40 ml) lemon juice

2 tbsp + 2 tsp (40 ml) lime juice

2 tbsp (30 ml) agave syrup

1 tsp your favorite hot sauce

Preheat the oven to 375°F (190°C).

Toss the corn kernels in a bowl with the oil and sprinkle with sea salt and coarse black pepper. Mix it all together and place the kernels on a parchment paper lined baking sheet. Roast in the oven, mixing every couple of minutes, for 9 to 11 minutes, or until the kernels are just beginning to brown in spots. Remove from the oven and let cool.

Mix the corn, quinoa, peppers, jalapeño, basil, green onion and 1 teaspoon of salt together in a large bowl. In a small bowl, whisk together the lemon juice, lime juice, agave and hot sauce. Pour the dressing over the top of the salad and fold it together with a spatula.

Let the salad rest for 30 minutes before serving for the flavors to meld.

Mango-Pomegranate Guacamole

While this guac would certainly be comfortable as a trendy topping for avocado toast, we love to keep it within arm's reach along with crisp nacho chips.

. . . .

3 or 4 avocados, ripe but not too soft

¼ cup (60 ml) lime juice

½ cup (75 g) diced sweet onion

1 small jalapeño pepper, minced (with seeds)

1 tsp Mexican chili powder

½ tsp ancho or chipotle chili powder

¼ tsp hot sauce

1 mango, peeled and diced

1 pomegranate, seeds only (see note)

⅓ cup (14 g) chopped fresh basil

½ tsp sea salt

¼ tsp freshly ground pepper

Pit and cube the avocados, and coarsely mash them with the lime juice in a large bowl. We like to leave a bit of chunk to the avocado. Add the onion, jalapeño, chili powders and hot sauce, and fold everything together with a spatula.

Add the mango, pomegranate seeds, basil, salt and pepper and fold everything together. Check the guac for seasoning and adjust if necessary.

Note: If you're not serving this guac right away, do not add the pomegranate seeds as they'll discolor the avocado. Fold them in right before serving. To remove the seeds from the pomegranate, cut the pomegranate along its equator. Working over a strainer set in the sink, hold a pomegranate half in your hand with the cut side facing down and firmly tap the pomegranate with the back of a wooden spoon to dislodge the seeds. Remove any white pith that falls into the strainer.

Chapter 5

POUR 'EM ON THICK!

Sensational Sauces, Salsas and Chutneys

Suffice it to say that I love getting saucy. Most of these recipes were originally created as toppings for my favorite dish—roasted Yukon Gold potatoes. It's not wrong to love a yellow-fleshed spud, is it?

Cashew Sour Cream

We love Cashew Sour Cream, and, as you've seen, we use it in or on many of our recipes. A high-speed blender is essential to reach the smooth and creamy texture of sour cream. You can also freeze this sour cream in a tightly sealed container for up to 3 months.

Makes approximately 2½ cups (600 ml)

2 cups (300 g) raw cashews, soaked (see note)

1 cup (240 ml) water

3 tbsp (45 ml) apple cider vinegar

2 tbsp (30 ml) lemon juice

½ tsp Himalayan pink sea salt

Drain the cashews, rinse well and drain again.

Place the cashews and all of the remaining ingredients in a high-speed blender and blend on high until the mixture is smooth and creamy. Scrape down the sides of the blender a couple of times along the way.

Add additional water, 1 tablespoon (15 ml) at a time, if necessary, to reach your desired consistency.

Tightly cover and refrigerate the Cashew Sour Cream for up to 1 week or freeze it for up to 3 months.

Note: Soak the cashews in water for a minimum of 6 hours—overnight is better. If you're pressed for time, you can boil the cashews. Bring a pot of water to a boil and add the cashews. Boil for 10 minutes. Remove from the heat and let the cashews remain in the pot for an additional 10 minutes. Drain and rinse well under cold water, then proceed with the recipe.

Peanut Sauce

This was my very first peanut sauce, and it still remains my favorite. It's a perfect satay sauce; it's a superb gado-gado sauce; it's a great sauce over our Chick*n Schnitzel (page 14) . . . or you can just eat it by the spoonful!

1 cup (150 g) raw peanuts

¼ cup (45 g) red pepper, chopped

1 tbsp (15 ml) grape-seed or canola oil

1 tbsp (14 g) Thai red curry paste (see note)

2 cloves garlic, minced

½ tsp minced Thai red chili

¼ tsp white pepper

3 tbsp (28 g) brown sugar

1 (14-oz [400-ml]) can coconut milk

2 tbsp (30 ml) rice vinegar

1 tbsp (15 ml) vegan oyster sauce

Toast the peanuts in a dry pan, stirring often, over medium-low heat for 6 to 8 minutes or until golden. Remove the toasted peanuts to a bowl and allow them to cool. When cool, add the peanuts to a food processor and pulse to a medium-fine grain. Do not over-pulse or you'll end up with peanut butter. Remove the ground peanuts to a bowl and set aside.

Wipe out the processor and add the red pepper, oil, curry paste, garlic, chili and pepper. Pulse the mixture to a smooth paste.

Add the pepper paste mixture to a wok over medium heat and cook, stirring constantly, for approximately 5 minutes or until the paste has darkened and is very fragrant. Add the brown sugar and continue stirring for 4 to 5 minutes or until the sugar has dissolved. Add the ground peanuts and continue stirring until the peanuts are well coated with the paste.

Reduce the heat to simmer, and gradually whisk in the coconut milk, vinegar and oyster sauce. Whisk until the mixture is fully incorporated and then let it simmer for 15 minutes. Do not let the sauce boil.

This sauce can be served hot or at room temperature. If you refrigerate it, the sauce will thicken. Simply reheat the sauce over low heat until it has regained its original consistency.

Note: Check the ingredients of the Thai red curry paste to make sure it is vegan. Some curry pastes contain fish sauce.

Mozzarella Cheeze

Mild flavored, shred-able, melt-able, brown-able and perfect for any recipe that calls for mozz. Wrapped in plastic wrap, this cheeze lasts for 14 days in the refrigerator.

¾ cup (115 g) raw cashew pieces

¾ cup (180 ml) unsweetened almond milk

1¾ cups (420 ml) water, divided

2 tsp (10 ml) tahini

3 tbsp (45 ml) lemon juice

¼ cup (60 ml) coconut oil, melted

4½ tsp (11 g) onion powder

1 tsp sea salt

¾ tsp garlic powder

¼ tsp dried basil

2 tbsp + 1½ tsp (30 g) agar-agar powder (do not use agar flakes)

Prepare the cheeze molds. Silicone molds work great if you have them. At YamChops, we use mini loaf pans lightly brushed with olive oil as our cheeze molds.

Add the cashews, almond milk, ½ cup (120 ml) of water, tahini, lemon juice, coconut oil, onion powder, salt, garlic powder and basil to a high-speed blender. Blend until smooth, scraping down the sides of the blender a couple of times.

Place the agar agar powder and 1¼ cups (300 ml) of water in a pot over medium heat. Whisk regularly until the mixture just begins to bubble. Reduce the heat to simmer and cook, whisking constantly, for 1 minute or until the mixture just starts to thicken.

Immediately remove the agar agar mixture from the heat and empty it into the blender with the other ingredients, scraping the sides and bottom of the pot with a spatula. Blend on high until the mixture is completely smooth.

Working quickly, pour the cheeze into the prepared molds, cover with plastic wrap and refrigerate. Allow the cheeze to set up for a minimum of 4 hours.

Butternut Squash Cheeze Sauce

Makes about 2 cups (480 ml)

We use this cheeze sauce on darn near everything: in our Butternut Squash Cheeze 'n' Mac Casserole (page 49), as a topping on nacho chips, draped over roasted Yukon Gold potato wedges, smothered on roasted cauliflower, mixed in a celery root mash . . . ya see? Darn near everything!

3¼ cups (453 g) butternut squash, peeled and cut in 1-inch (25-mm) cubes

1 small sweet onion, peeled and cut in 1-inch (25-mm) cubes

1 large clove garlic

⅔ cup (100 g) raw cashews

¾ cup (177 ml) unsweetened almond milk

3 tbsp (38 g) roasted red pepper, chopped

2 tbsp (29 g) white miso

1 tbsp (15 ml) tamari or soy sauce

2 tsp (10 ml) apple cider vinegar

2 tsp (10 g) sea salt

1 tsp Hungarian paprika

½ tsp white pepper

⅛ tsp cayenne pepper

Bring a pot with 2 inches (50 mm) of water to a boil over high heat. Place the butternut squash, onion and garlic in a steamer basket, and place the basket in the pot. Cover the pot. Steam for 15 to 20 minutes or until the squash can be easily pierced with a skewer. Place the squash, onions and garlic in a high-speed blender.

Bring a pot of water to a boil, add the cashews and boil for 10 minutes. Turn the heat off and let the cashews rest in the hot water for an additional 10 minutes. Rinse the cashews in a strainer and add to the blender with the butternut squash. Add the almond milk, roasted red pepper, miso, tamari, vinegar, salt, paprika, white pepper and cayenne pepper to the blender.

Blend on high speed, scraping down the sides a couple of times along the way, until the sauce is smooth and creamy.

Tightly sealed, this sauce will last for up to 2 weeks in the refrigerator.

Chipotle Mayo

We can't count the number of things that we use our Chipotle Mayo on. Well, we probably could, but do you really care? Suffice it to say that this quick sauce is versatile and delicious!

Makes about 1 cup (220 ml)

. . . .

1 cup (220 g) vegan mayo

1–2 tbsp (10–20 g) minced chipotle in adobo

2 tsp (10 ml) lime juice

¼ tsp sea salt

Place all of the ingredients in the bowl of a food processor and blend until smooth.

Adjust the heat level by adding more minced chipotle in adobo until you reach your preferred Scoville scale. At YamChops, we add 1½ tablespoons (16 g) of minced chipotle in adobo and 1 teaspoon of the liquid.

Tightly sealed, this sauce will last for up to 2 weeks in the refrigerator.

Sriracha Aioli

Comes together in the blink of an eye, and is the perfect topping for our No-Crab Crab Cakes (page 38)—or burgers—or sandwiches—or potato wedges.

Makes about 1 ½ cups (330 ml)

. . . .

1 cup (220 g) vegan mayo

1 tbsp (12 g) evaporated cane sugar

1 tbsp (15 ml) Dijon mustard

2 tsp (10 ml) Sriracha

2 tsp (15 g) minced ginger

2 tsp (10 ml) lemon juice

1 tsp rice vinegar

¼ tsp sea salt

Large pinch white pepper

Place all of the ingredients in the bowl of a mini food processor and blend until smooth. Tightly sealed, this aioli will last for up to 2 weeks in the refrigerator.

Mushroom-Shallot Gravy

Eat. More. Gravy.

This gravy may be left chunky or you can blend it smooth in your blender.

. . . .

2 tbsp (30 g) vegan butter

1 cup (150 g) diced cremini mushrooms

½ cup (50 g) diced shallot

1 tbsp (8 g) unbleached all-purpose flour

¾ cup (180 ml) vegetable stock

½ cup (120 ml) unsweetened almond milk

2 tsp (10 ml) tamari or soy sauce

½ tsp cracked black pepper

¼ tsp red chili flakes

Melt the butter in a large skillet over medium heat. Add the mushrooms and shallots, and sauté for 7 to 8 minutes or until the mushrooms begin to give off their liquid.

Sprinkle the flour over the mushroom mixture and continue to sauté, stirring constantly, for 3 minutes. Slowly whisk in the stock, almond milk and tamari. Bring the mixture to a soft boil and reduce the heat to low. Stir in the pepper and chili flakes.

Cook the gravy, whisking constantly, for 2 to 3 minutes or until the gravy thickens.

Serve chunky or carefully add the mixture to a blender and blend until it's smooth. Tightly sealed, this gravy will last for up to 1 week in the refrigerator.

Soy-Mirin Glaze

If Hunan Dumplings (page 80) and Soy-Mirin Glaze were subscribed to the same dating service, they'd swipe right.

Makes about 1½ cups (360 ml)

½ cup (120 ml) mirin

½ cup (96 g) evaporated cane sugar

¼ cup (60 ml) sweet soy sauce (also called ketjap manis)

¼ cup (60 ml) tamari or soy sauce

2 tsp (6 g) minced garlic

2 tsp (9 g) minced ginger

Combine all of the ingredients in a pot over medium-low heat. Cook for approximately 8 minutes or until the sauce has thickened slightly and coats the back of a spoon. Covered, this sauce will last for 2 weeks in the refrigerator.

Mango Salsa

Heap a tablespoon (10 g) of this Mango Salsa in the center of a bowl of Black Bean Soup (page 101). It's a match made in soup heaven!

Makes about 1 cup (160 g)

1 ripe but firm mango, diced into ⅛-inch (3-mm) pieces

2 tbsp (30 ml) fresh lime juice

1 tbsp (3 g) chopped fresh basil

1 tbsp (3 g) chopped fresh mint

2 tsp (6 g) brown sugar

¾ tsp minced jalapeño

Pinch salt

Mix all of the salsa ingredients together in a bowl until the sugar has dissolved.

Allow to rest at room temperature for 30 minutes for the flavors to meld. This salsa will last for 3 days in the refrigerator.

Shiitake Miso Gravy

Love, love, love this gravy over our Beet Wellington (page 17). It's also great over mashed potatoes or vegan poutine. Hey, we're Canadian eh, we know poutine! Interesting fact: In most Canadian households, poutine is the first solid food fed to babies!

3 tbsp (45 ml) olive oil, divided

1 tbsp (8 g) all-purpose flour or all-purpose gluten-free flour

½ cup (50 g) chopped shallots

1 cup (150 g) chopped fresh shiitake mushrooms, stems removed

1½ cups (360 ml) vegetable stock

2 tsp (10 ml) mushroom soy sauce

¼ tsp white pepper

1 tbsp (15 g) white miso

Prepare the roux by heating 1 tablespoon (15 ml) of oil in a small pot over medium heat. Sprinkle the flour over the oil and, whisking constantly, cook for 4 to 5 minutes, until the mixture is golden in color and smells a bit nutty. Remove the pot from the heat and set the roux aside until needed.

Heat the remaining oil in a pot over medium heat. Add the shallots and sauté for 2 minutes. Add the mushrooms and continue to sauté, stirring regularly, for an additional 3 minutes.

Raise the heat to high and add the stock, mushroom soy sauce and white pepper. Bring the mixture to a boil and immediately turn the heat down to low. Add the roux that you prepared earlier and whisk it in completely. You don't want any lumps.

Simmer the gravy, whisking regularly, for approximately 7 to 10 minutes or until it has thickened slightly. Remove the pot from the heat and whisk in the miso until it has completely dissolved.

Carefully purée the gravy in batches in a blender until it is smooth. Transfer the gravy to a clean pot and keep warm over very low heat until you're ready to serve. Tightly sealed, this gravy will last for up to 1 week in the refrigerator.

Meatless Meat Sauce

Of course, we serve our meat sauce ladled over spaghetti . . . and we regularly top our Chick*n Fried Baked Portobello (page 66) with it too. Generously top a Chick*n Schnitzel (page 14) or a Pinto Bean Cutlet (page 54) with shredded Mozzarella Cheese (page 144) and bake it until the cheeze is ooey and gooey. Spoon on a couple of tablespoons of warmed Meatless Meat Sauce and try to make it to the table without sneaking a bite.

2 tbsp (30 ml) olive oil

1 cup (136 g) ¼-inch (6-mm) diced sweet onion

2 large cloves garlic, minced

1 (406 g) package your favorite veggie ground round (we use Gardein, or for a soy-free/allergen-free version, we use Big Mountain's Cauli Crumble)

1 (28-oz [806-ml]) can diced tomatoes

1 cup (240 ml) water

2 tbsp (30 g) tomato paste

1 tbsp (10 g) brown sugar

1½ tsp (1 g) dried basil

1 tsp dried parsley

1 tsp sea salt

¼ tsp freshly ground black pepper

¼ tsp red chili flakes

¼ cup (60 ml) red wine (see note)

Heat the olive oil in a Dutch oven or soup pot over medium heat. When hot, add the onion and sauté for 4 to 5 minutes until translucent. Add the garlic and the veggie ground round, and continue to sauté for 5 minutes, stirring often. Add the tomatoes and water, and with a spoon, scrape up the packed-full-of-flavor browned bits that have stuck to the bottom of the pot. Continue to cook, mixing regularly, for approximately 10 minutes or until the sauce begins to boil.

Turn the heat down to simmer, add the tomato paste, sugar, basil, parsley, salt, pepper and chili flakes to the pot. Stir everything together and let the sauce simmer for 30 minutes. Give it a mix from time to time.

Add the red wine. Stir well and continue to simmer for an additional 30 minutes.

Note: Pick a red wine you enjoy. Remember, if you wouldn't drink it, don't cook with it. But, hey, you get to finish the rest of the bottle with dinner.

Pickled Avocado

Makes 1 (750-ml) jar

Truth be told, this recipe kinda happened by accident. I was looking for a way to extend the life of the avocado on our lunch counter and came up with the idea of pickling it. Who'd have thought that it would become our most requested condiment!

1½ cups (360 ml) water

1 cup (240 ml) white wine vinegar

2 tbsp (30 ml) agave syrup

1 tbsp (15 g) kosher salt

1 tbsp (9 g) whole black peppercorns

2 tsp (1 g) red chili flakes

3 small cloves garlic, thinly sliced

¼-inch (6-mm) thick slice of lemon

2 avocados, ripe but firm

Bring the water, vinegar, agave and salt to a boil in a medium pot over medium heat, whisking gently for 4 to 5 minutes until the salt dissolves. Remove the pot from the heat and set the pickling liquid aside to cool completely.

Thoroughly clean a 750-ml (1-quart) pickling jar and lid. Place the peppercorns, chili flakes, garlic and lemon in the bottom of the jar.

Peel and pit the avocados and cut it into ½-inch (13-mm) cubes. Add the avocado cubes to the jar. Pour the cooled pickling liquid over the avocado to fill the jar to within ¼ inch (6 mm) of the rim. Wipe the rim clean and seal the jar.

Refrigerate for a minimum of 4 hours before using. Refrigerated and sealed, this pickle lasts for 2 weeks. But we promise you, once you try it, it won't last nearly that long.

Parsley-Mint Chimichurri

Makes about 1 ½ cups (230 g)

Fresh and full of herb flavor, this chimichurri will surprise and delight you with its smoky and spicy undertones. Spoon it on our Butternut Squash Steak (page 46) to take them to never-before-reached heights.

1 cup (25 g) loosely packed fresh flat leaf parsley

¼ cup (6 g) loosely packed fresh mint leaves

1 small clove garlic, chopped

2 tsp (6 g) chopped jalapeño

½ lemon, juiced

¼ tsp sea salt

⅛ tsp hickory liquid smoke

⅛ tsp freshly ground black pepper

¼ cup (60 ml) olive oil

Place the parsley, mint, garlic and jalapeño in a high-speed blender, and pulse the mixture a few times to roughly chop the herbs. Add the lemon juice, salt, liquid smoke and pepper, and pulse a couple more times to combine.

With the processor running on low speed, slowly stream in the olive oil. Continue to process, scraping down the sides a couple of times along the way, until the chimichurri is smooth.

Mango Tamarind Chutney

Dedicate a lazy Sunday afternoon to making a batch of this chutney. The recipe yields enough to share with your friends and still have plenty for yourself. Refrigerated, the chutney keeps for at least 3 months, but I promise you it won't last that long. It's wonderful served with Indian food, and it has a home away from home on a vegan cheeze and crackers platter.

Regardless of the fact that this recipe has 20 ingredients and takes upwards of 90 minutes, it really is as easy as 1–2–3, and it makes a chutney that'll blow up your taste buds.

4 ripe but firm mangos, peeled and diced into ¼-inch (6-mm) pieces

2 cups (300 g) diced sweet onion, diced into ¼-inch (6-mm) pieces

2 cups (220 g) brown sugar

¾ cup (150 g) evaporated cane sugar

1½ cups (360 ml) white vinegar

1 cup (150 g) golden raisins

1 cup (120 g) dried cranberries

3 tbsp (43 g) minced ginger

3 tbsp (43 g) tamarind paste

3 small cloves garlic, minced

Zest of 1 lemon

2 tbsp (18 g) brown mustard seeds

2 tbsp (15 g) ground cinnamon

1 tbsp (2 g) dried red chili flakes

2 tsp (10 g) sea salt

2 tsp (5 g) ground cloves

½ tsp cayenne pepper

2 bananas, puréed

2 mangos, puréed

½ cup (30 g) unsweetened shredded coconut

Sterilize the canning jars and lids by placing them on a rack set in a deep pot. Cover the jars with hot water and bring the water to a boil. Boil the jars and lids for 15 minutes. Turn off the heat and let the jars stand in the hot water until needed.

Place the mango pieces, onion, sugars, vinegar, raisins, cranberries, ginger, tamarind paste, garlic, lemon zest, mustard seeds, cinnamon, chili flakes, salt, cloves and pepper in a large pot over medium heat and stir to combine. Stirring regularly, bring the mixture to a boil. Reduce the heat to low, and simmer the mixture for 45 minutes. Give it a stir every 5 minutes or so.

At the 45-minute mark, add the banana, mango purée and coconut to the pot and stir to combine. Continue to cook for 30 to 45 minutes or until the mixture thickens to a chutney-like consistency.

Fill the prepared canning jars. Carefully remove the jars from the water and invert on a towel to dry. The jars should be hot when filling them. Fill the jars to approximately ½ inch (13 mm) below the rim. Wipe the rims clean and seal the jars. Return the filled jars to the pot of hot water. Bring the water back to a boil and boil the filled jars for an additional 10 minutes. Carefully remove the jars and set them aside to cool.

Sweet-and-Spicy Tomato Jam

Makes 6 (250-ml) jars

It's a little bit sweet and a little bit spicy and a whole lotta tomatoey! We love this jam spread on crackers or as a burger topping, and it's an indispensible component of our vegan cheeze platters!

3 lb (1.3 kg) ripe tomatoes

2 cups (400 g) sugar

¼ cup (60 ml) lime juice

¼ cup (15 g) finely chopped ginger

1½ tsp (1 g) red chili flakes

1½ tsp (4 g) ground cumin

1½ tsp (4 g) ground cinnamon

1½ tsp (8 g) sea salt

¼ tsp ground cloves

Sterilize the canning jars and lids by placing them on a rack set in a deep pot. Cover the jars with hot water and bring the water to a boil. Boil the jars and lids for 15 minutes. Turn off the heat and let the jars stand in the hot water until needed.

Core and chop the tomatoes in ½-inch (13-mm) pieces. Place the tomatoes, sugar, lime juice, ginger, chili flakes, cumin, cinnamon, salt and cloves in a large pot over medium high heat. Bring the mixture to a boil, stirring often.

Turn the heat to low and simmer for 60 to 75 minutes or until the jam has thickened. The cooking time will vary based on the amount of water in your tomatoes. Stir the mixture often.

Remove the jam from the heat. Carefully remove the jars from the water and invert on a towel to dry. The jars should be hot when filling them. Fill the jars to approximately ½ inch (13 mm) below the rim. Wipe the rims clean and seal the jars. Return the filled jars to the pot of hot water. Bring the water back to a boil and boil the filled jars for an additional 10 minutes. Carefully remove the jars and set them aside to cool.

Store the tomato jam in the refrigerator for up to 60 days.

Hemp Parm

Makes about 1½ cups (270 g)

We shake this stuff on everything. It's the perfect finishing sprinkle for our Kale Caesar! Bowl (page 110) or as a topping for a heaping bowl of pasta or Chick*n Fried Baked Portobello (page 66) or lasagna.

1¼ cups (57 g) nutritional yeast

¼ cup (40 g) hemp seeds

1 tsp sea salt

½ tsp coarse grind pepper (sometimes called butcher's grind)

¼ tsp turmeric powder

Place all of the ingredients in a bowl and mix together well. Hemp Parm lasts for 30 days if kept in a sealed jar.

Chapter 6

CHOCOLATE

Simple and Simply Scrumptious
Chocolate Endings

Yup—nothing but our chocolate faves. Is it obvious that I have lived with three women for the majority of my cooking career?

Chocolate-Banana Cream Pie

This smooth and silky pie showcases chocolate and bananas in perfect harmony. And, it's sugar-free to boot!

. . . .

Crust
1 cup (175 g) Medjool dates

1¼ cups (155 g) walnuts

2 tsp (30 ml) melted coconut oil

½ tsp sea salt

¼ tsp ancho chili powder

Filling
2 (260-g) packages firm silken tofu (see note)

¾ tsp vanilla

⅛ tsp sea salt

2¾ cups (480 g) dark or semi-sweet vegan chocolate chips

2 bananas, sliced in ⅛-inch (3-mm) rounds, plus more for serving

Date sugar or raw sugar, for sprinkling

Note: Always search out non-GMO tofu for tofu recipes.

To prepare the crust, pit the dates and soak them in warm water for 15 minutes. Drain the dates and add them to a food processor. Pulse them until they are small bits and they ball together.

Remove the dates from the processor and add the walnuts. Pulse the walnuts until they are coarsely chopped. Add the dates back into the processor along with the coconut oil, sea salt and chili powder. Pulse the mixture until everything is well mixed. Test the consistency of the crust by pressing it between your fingers. The crust should stick together, yet still be pliable enough to form into a pie plate. If it's too dry, add another processed date or two. If it's too wet, add another 1 to 2 tablespoons (7 to 14 g) of pulsed walnuts.

Place the mixture into a 9-inch (200-mm) pie plate lined with plastic wrap. Press the crust flat with your fingers and shape it to the form of the bottom and sides of the pie plate. Place the crust in the freezer for 30 minutes to set.

Preheat the oven to broil. Set a pot with 2 inches (50 mm) of water to boil.

Add the silken tofu to the processor along with the vanilla and sea salt. Pulse the mixture a few times to break up the tofu.

Place the chocolate chips in a bowl large enough to sit on top of the pot of boiling water. You do not want the bottom of the bowl to touch the boiling water. Place the bowl on top of the pot (double boiler style) and melt the chocolate chips, stirring with a silicone spatula, until they are a smooth and creamy chocolate lake. Be careful when touching the bowl—it will get hot!

Pour the melted chocolate into the processor with the tofu and process the mixture until it is super smooth.

Place the sliced bananas on a parchment paper lined baking sheet and sprinkle them with sugar. Place the baking sheet in the oven to caramelize the sugar, approximately 30 to 45 seconds. Keep an eye on them—burnt sugar can be super bitter!

Remove the crust from the freezer and lay the caramelized bananas over the bottom, stretching up the sides. Grab the chocolate cream mixture and carefully pour it over the bananas to fill the pie shell. Smooth the top with an offset spatula or the back of a spoon.

Lightly cover the pie with plastic wrap and refrigerate it for 4 hours to set up. Set a few toothpicks in the pie to keep the plastic wrap from touching the surface of the pie. Slice and serve with a couple of fresh banana slices on top as a garnish.

Rocky Road Fudge

What started out as a topping for our coconut ice cream sundae quickly turned into our best-selling packaged sweet treat. The first time I made this fudge at home, my wife polished it off (all of it) in less than 30 hours, and every time we make it at YamChops, there's a line of staff waiting and hoping for any offcuts.

. . . .

⅔ cup (160 ml) coconut milk

2 tbsp (30 ml) coconut oil

2 cups (350 g) semi-sweet vegan chocolate chips

1 tsp pure vanilla extract

¼ tsp pure mint extract

1 cup (50 g) vegan mini marshmallows (see note)

½ cup (58 g) walnut pieces

Line a baking sheet with parchment paper and set aside.

Heat the coconut milk in a medium-size pot over medium heat, stirring constantly, and bring to a very low simmer. Adjust the heat to maintain this very low simmer for 2 minutes. You don't want the coconut milk to boil.

Add the coconut oil and stir for 3 to 4 minutes, or until it has melted and is fully incorporated. Add the chocolate chips and stir for approximately 8 minutes, until they are fully melted and the mixture is silky smooth.

Remove the pot from the heat, and working quickly, stir in the vanilla and mint extracts. Add the marshmallows and walnuts, and stir until they are evenly distributed. Pour the fudge onto the prepared baking sheet. Using an offset or silicone spatula, spread the fudge into a rectangle about ⅜- to ½-inch (9- to 13-mm) thick.

Put the pan in the freezer and freeze the fudge for a minimum of 4 hours or until fully hardened.

Cut or break the fudge into pieces and go for it. Keep the remaining fudge (if any) refrigerated.

Note: We prefer Dandies brand marshmallows. If you can only find vegan full-size marshmallows, cut them into quarters before adding them to the recipe.

Chocolate-Almond Pudding

Smooth and creamy! Creamy and smooth, with a hint of orange.

• •

6 tbsp (57 g) cornstarch mixed with 5 tbsp (75 ml) cold water

½ cup + 1 tbsp (114 g) evaporated cane sugar

½ cup (56 g) cocoa powder

Large pinch of sea salt

4 cups (946 ml) unsweetened almond milk

⅔ cup (112 g) semi-sweet vegan chocolate chips

1 tsp vanilla extract

¼ tsp orange essence

Whisk the cornstarch and water together in a small bowl and set aside.

Set a pot over medium heat and add the sugar, cocoa powder and salt, mixing well to combine. Slowly add the almond milk, whisking constantly, until the mixture is smooth. Cook, stirring regularly, for approximately 10 minutes, or until a very thin film forms on the surface and wisps of steam begin to rise from the pot.

Add the chocolate chips, vanilla and orange essence, and continue to whisk for 7 to 8 minutes until the chips have melted and the mixture is silky smooth.

Give the cornstarch slurry a quick whisk and slowly add it to the pudding, whisking constantly until the pudding has thickened. This only takes a couple of minutes.

Immediately remove the pot from the heat and transfer it to serving bowls. Cover the bowls with plastic wrap and refrigerate for a minimum of 4 hours.

Two things: 1) This pudding is outstanding topped with fresh berries and some vegan whipped cream; 2) It's okay to lick the bowl before washing it.

Cauliflower Chocolate Pudding

We've all heard it: Eat more veggies! We can't think of a better way to supersize your daily veggie fix than with this plant-based, sugar-free, smooth and creamy chocolate pudding. A bowl of this creamy goodness topped with fresh blueberries and a spoon of vegan whipped cream—now, that's what we're talking about.

• •

3 cups (385 g) cauliflower florets

1¼ cups (300 ml) unsweetened almond milk or other plant-based milk, divided

⅓ cup (35 g) cocoa powder

10 Medjool dates, pitted

1 tbsp (15 ml) maple syrup

1 tsp vanilla extract

Wash the cauliflower and break it into small florets. Set up a steamer by bringing 2 inches (50 mm) of water to a simmer in a pot. Place the cauliflower in a steamer basket, place the basket in a pot, cover the pot and steam the cauliflower for approximately 15 minutes, until it is very tender and easily pierced with a toothpick.

Add the steamed cauliflower to a high-speed blender along with 1 cup (240 ml) of the almond milk, the cocoa powder, dates, maple syrup and vanilla. Blend on high speed until smooth and creamy, adding the additional ¼ cup (60 ml) of almond milk, if necessary, to reach your desired consistency.

Refrigerated, this pudding will last for 5 days.

Pumpkin Brownie Loaf

Makes 12 mini loaves or 1 large loaf

What started out as dessert for a holiday meal has turned into a year-round offering. Simply put, it's a chocolate brownie cake with a layer of pumpkin pie on top. Can't go wrong with that combo!

. . . .

Brownie

1 cup (240 ml) canned puréed pumpkin

½ cup (100 g) sugar

¼ cup (60 ml) melted coconut oil

1 tsp vanilla

¾ cup (96 g) unbleached all-purpose flour

⅔ cup (115 g) semi-sweet vegan chocolate chips

3 tbsp (21 g) cocoa powder

1 tbsp (15 g) arrowroot starch

½ tsp baking powder

½ tsp baking soda

¼ tsp sea salt

Pumpkin

1 cup (240 ml) canned puréed pumpkin

½ cup (120 ml) unsweetened almond milk

1 tsp vanilla

¼ cup (50 g) sugar

2 tbsp (30 g) arrowroot starch

1 tsp pumpkin pie spice

Raw unsalted pepitas, for garnish

Preheat the oven to 350°F (177°C). Lightly oil 12 mini loaf pans or an 8 × 8 inch (200 × 200 mm) baking pan.

To prepare the brownie, whisk together the pumpkin, sugar, coconut oil and vanilla in a large bowl. In a separate bowl, mix together the flour, chocolate chips, cocoa powder, arrowroot starch, baking powder, baking soda and salt. Add the dry ingredients to the bowl containing the brownie mixture and mix well.

To prepare the pumpkin, whisk together the pumpkin, almond milk and vanilla in a large bowl. Add the sugar, arrowroot starch and pumpkin pie spice, and mix well.

Fill the prepared mini loaf pans two-thirds full with the brownie mixture and smooth the surface with the back of a teaspoon. Fill the remainder of the loaf pan with the pumpkin mixture. Sprinkle a few pepitas on top and place in the oven for 30 minutes or until a toothpick inserted in the center of the loaf comes out dry.

These brownies will last for 3 days in the refrigerator.

Black Bean Brownies

Rich and chewy-gooey good! These brownies are great as they are, but serving them warm with a scoop of coconut ice cream takes them over the top!

• •

1½ cups (250 g) black beans, rinsed

½ cup (48 g) quick oats

½ cup + 2 tbsp (150 ml) maple syrup

¼ cup (60 ml) melted coconut oil

7 tsp (17 g) cocoa powder

1 tbsp (15 ml) warm water

1½ tsp (8 ml) vanilla

½ tsp baking powder

½ cup (90 g) semi-sweet vegan chocolate chips

½ cup (65 g) chopped walnuts

Preheat the oven to 350°F (177°C). Lightly oil an 8 × 8 inch (200 × 200 mm) baking pan.

Place the black beans, oats, maple syrup, coconut oil, cocoa powder, water, vanilla and baking powder in the food processor and blend until the mixture is smooth. The mixture should be thick but pourable. If the mixture is too thick, add another tablespoon (15 ml) of water. Remove the black bean mixture to a large bowl and fold in the chocolate chips and the walnuts.

Pour the mixture into the prepared baking pan, smooth the surface with an offset spatula or the back of a spoon, and bake for 15 to 17 minutes, or until the surface of the brownies begins to crack and a toothpick inserted in the middle comes out clean.

Remove the pan from the oven, and let the brownies cool for 15 minutes before cutting them.

ACKNOWLEDGMENTS

While this cookbook carries the YamChops name, it wouldn't have come to be were it not for hundreds of people that played a part in this journey. I'll highlight a few and honor the many.

My wife Toni and daughters, Jess and Leya—thank you for making this dream come true.

Will and Elizabeth of Page Street Publishing—thank you for publishing this cookbook and for patiently answering my never-ending stream of questions.

To everyone that has wondered, "What the heck is a vegan butcher shop?" and have come by YamChops to find out—your support and your enthusiasm are the reasons we do what we do. Thank you.

Scott and Lawrence, our partners in Vancouver—thank you for sharing our dream and our passion.

Our amazing team of Yambassadors in Toronto and Vancouver, past, present and future—thank you for raising the bar.

Nigel, Dror and Tonino—thank you for your mentoring and your coaching . . . and for being there when we didn't know where to turn.

To a very special company in Ann Arbor, Michigan, Zingerman's—thank you for the lessons you've taught us.

A giant virtual hug goes out to the thousands of people around the world who have sent us messages of support.

Tina Louise, a very special cop in Toronto—thank you.

To my mom, who said for years, "Mikey—you really should write a cookbook." While you did get to see us open YamChops, I'm sorry you didn't get to see this cookbook come to life.

And to my family and friends—thank you for loving my food and supporting my dream.

ABOUT THE AUTHOR

Plant-based for more than four decades, Michael Abramson is an adman turned vegan butcher. Prior to opening North America's first vegan butcher shop, Michael owned theadlibgroup, a boutique marketing agency in Toronto with a specialty in the food and franchise industries.

Michael's superpowers include innovation, recipe development, marketing, creativity and team leadership. During the years at the agency, Michael and Toni invested in education in transformative thinking and business management, effectively creating an "un-agency" with integrity as its foundation. theadlibgroup went far beyond the traditional deliverables of advertising, marketing, social media and PR to include event development, innovation and ideation, creative coaching and a true hands-on involvement in the business of its clients.

Michael's passion for plant-based cuisine continued to grow, and when he and Toni sold the agency in 2012, Michael's "little red sports car" was YamChops.

INDEX